A taste of
CHOCOLATE

Published by Grenadine Publishing 2011
Grenadine Publishing is an imprint of Massolit Publishing Ltd.

A Taste of Chocolate
© Stevali Production, Örjan Westerlund and Eliq Maranik 2011

First edition
ISBN: 978-1-908233-08-0

Original title: Choklad – kunskap ger mersmak
Translated from the Swedish by Katarina Trodden

Graphic design: Stevali Production

All photos by Eliq Maranik / Stevali Production, except:
p. 4 – Fotolia / Liv Friis-Larsen
p. 10 – Esteban Agencies
p. 8, 11, 14, 15, 16, 27 – Maja Berthas
p. 10, 22 – www.valrhona.fr / J C Quinard
p. 6 – www.sxc.hu
p. 12, 24 – iStockphoto
p. 19 – Cloetta-Fazer AB

Printed in Italy by Jeming Srl 2011

Grenadine Publishing
6 Artichoke Mews
Artichoke Place
London SE5 8TS
United Kingdom
www.grenadine.se

A taste of CHOCOLATE

Örjan Westerlund & Eliq Maranik

GRENADINE

Contents

A Taste of Chocolate
– your first piece

How do you like your chocolate? Do you prefer eating creamy Lindt Petits Desserts in front of the television of a Thursday evening, or would you rather sit in the sun with a half-melted chocolate bar dug out from the bottom of your backpack? Maybe you are one of those people who refuses anything but a single piece, two at the most, of the darkest, most bitter and wonderfully fruity, tangy chocolate – a Michel Cluizel Maralumi from Papua New Guinea, for example?

Whichever category you belong to, we assume that you sink your teeth into a piece of chocolate with the same relish as when you were picking this book off the shelf.

We sincerely hope that it will offer you just the right blend of useful information and mouth-watering recipes.

This book will give you some idea of how cocoa is cultivated and how chocolate is manufactured. It also includes advice on what to drink with it and a few words concerning the beneficial effects of chocolate, all with the view of offering a deeper, richer experience. We hope you will enjoy many wonderful moments consuming the results of the recipes and that this book will inspire you to learn more.

Örjan Westerlund and Eliq Maranik

Birth of the Cocoa Bean

— *climate, growing conditions and types of cocoa*

Despite the fact that it can grow up to fifteen metres tall, the cocoa tree is a delicate thing. It needs to be sheltered from the wind, therefore it is often cultivated together with other crops such as banana, coffee or cassava and higher, more robust trees such as mahogany or species of Erythrina that offer shade. Commercially cultivated cocoa trees are not allowed to grow taller than 6–8 metres in order to make harvesting and maintenance easier.

The light-sensitive cocoa tree prefers conditions in which only 50–75 % of the sunlight filters through the foliage. The climate needs to be humid with an evenly distributed annual precipitation of around 1,500 millimetres and an average temperature of around 23 °C. Like tobacco and coffee, cocoa trees are cultivated between latitudes 18 degrees north and 15 degrees south. The best growing conditions are found at an altitude of 300 metres above sea level, sometimes higher, although never over 1,200 metres.

Cocoa trees are companion-planted with secondary crops such as banana or coffee, or spices such as vanilla or rosé pepper. It is a common misconception that these add flavour to the cocoa. This is impossible, however, since many of the crops, including cocoa, undergo fermentation and other flavour-enhancing processes after harvesting.

The cocoa tree flowers all year, and each tree yields between one and three hundred fruits a year, equivalent to between three and five kilos of cocoa beans. The number of flowers is frequently many thousand times greater than the number of fruits. The flowers grow directly from the tree trunk to which they are attached by a stalk. It takes four to eight months for flowers to develop into fruit.

The ripe fruit is harvested by hand by means of a knife with a long handle. Each pod is then split open and the pulp containing the seeds is scooped out and fermented. Each bean is the size of an almond. Depending on the type, each fruit contains between twenty and forty seeds.

DIFFERENT TYPES OF COCOA

The world's major cocoa producing nations are the Ivory Coast, Ghana, Indonesia, Cameroun, Nigeria and Brazil. Growers in Ecuador, Venezuela and the West Indies only produce one twentieth of the Ivory Coast record annual production of 1,300 kilotons, so the small producers are very small indeed in comparison.

The choice of bean is the basis for all chocolate production. There are three main types: Criollo Forastero and Trinitario.

◀ The cocoa tree flowers all year round and each tree yields between one and three hundred fruits per year.

9

The fruits of the cocoa tree are split open, the seeds are scooped out from the shell and then fermented. Each fruit yields 20–40 beans.

Criollo represents 5–7 per cent of the total world production. Criollo means 'creole' in Spanish, and this type of cocoa is mainly cultivated in Venezuela, Central America and Madagascar. Criollo is genetically divided into South American and Central American Criollo. It produces fewer, only twenty, beans per fruit; it is more prone to disease and more sensitive to climate changes than the other two. Criollo was the cocoa tree that Columbus and Cortès found when they arrived in the Americas in the 16th century. It is rich, fruity and smooth. A chocolate bar made from Criollo beans is reddish inside if you break it.

Forastero is the most common type in terms of volume with an 80 per cent share of the world market. It is mainly cultivated in Africa, where it was first introduced in 1822. It is also found in Central America. Forastero is a high yield type. Each fruit produces between forty and fifty beans. Forastero is less aromatic with a more acrid, bitter flavour. The fracture surface is black.

Trinitario is a Criollo/Forastero hybrid and represents about fifteen per cent of the world market. It is cultivated in, for example, Madagascar, Venezuela and the West Indies. Legend has it that it appeared after a hurricane devastated the Criollo plantations on Trinidad in 1727, after which Forastero trees were planted, with a third type of cocoa hybrid as a result. Trinitario has the advantage of having all the good properties inherent in both of its constituent parts, which means that it is resistant to disease, high yield, high in

THE COCOA BEAN

Theobromine is an alkaloid present in cocoa beans. It is highly poisonous to cats and dogs. Cats do not normally like chocolate, but dogs are happy to finish off a whole box if they are given the chance. Make sure never to leave chocolate out for the dog to find, it can be fatal.

fat, aromatic and easy to handle. In other words, it is a typical example of how one plus one makes three.

CHOCOLATE – NUTRITIONAL INFORMATION

Each cocoa bean weighs between 1 and 1.2 grams and is made up of:

50–55 % cocoa butter
20–25 % carbohydrates
15–20 % protein
5 % water
2.6 % minerals, e.g. zinc and magnesium
1.5 % theobromine
0.2 % caffeine

... it should be mentioned that one cup of hot chocolate contains approximately 20 mg, a cup of tea 70 mg and a cup of filter coffee 100 mg of caffeine. Naturally, you also need to add the love-inducing theobromine to the energy-boosting cocktail.

'Strength is the capacity to break a chocolate bar into four pieces with your bare hands – and then eat just one of the pieces.'

Judith Viorst

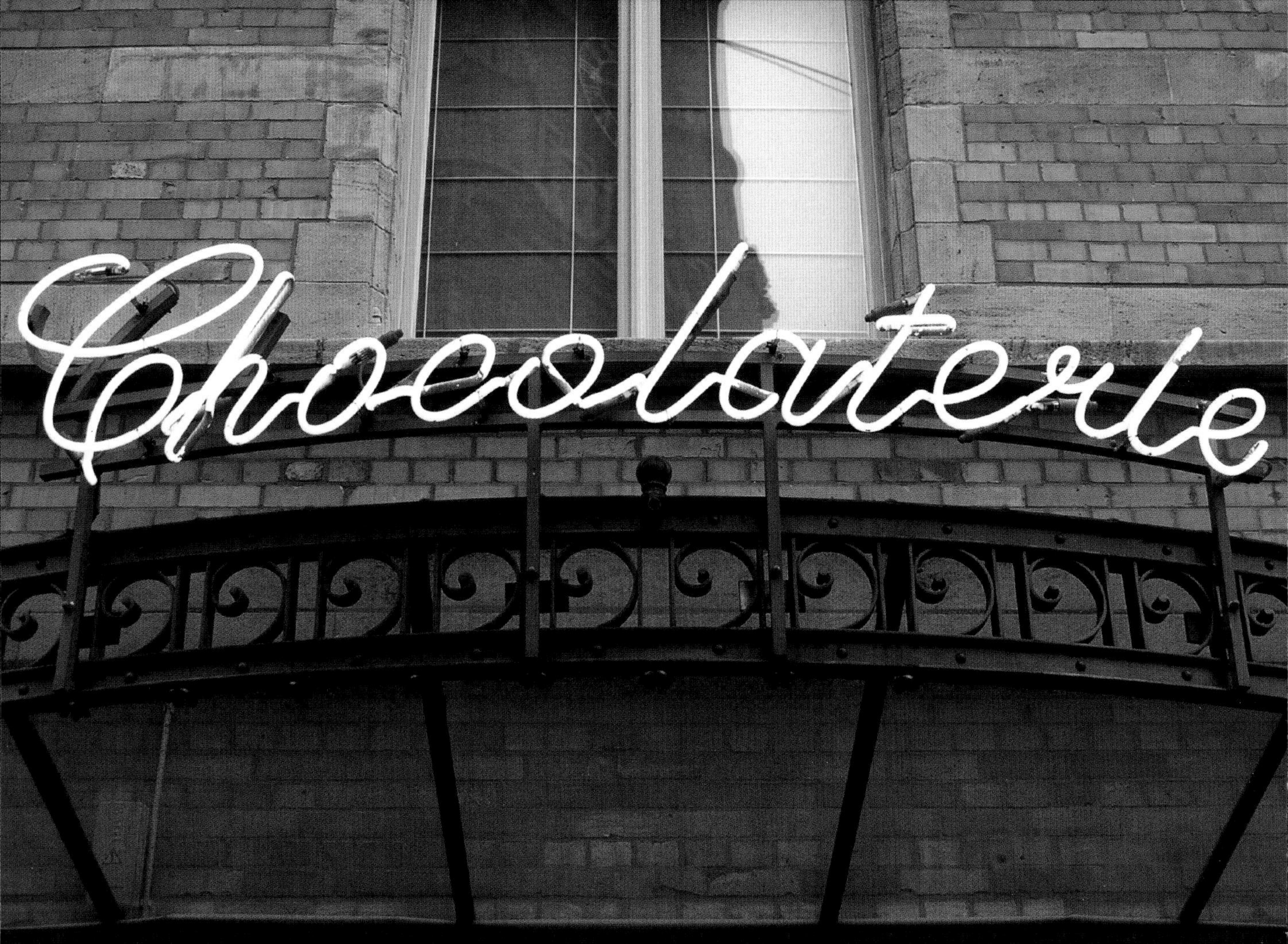
Chocolaterie

From Tree to Patisserie

Brewers have a tendency to boast about how much more complicated beer-making is compared to wine-making. You could argue that all a vintner needs to do is to tramp his grapes and they will ferment and turn into wine, while brewers need to produce fermentable sugar and then add yeast in order to get the brew started. In this respect, chocolate manufacturers have more to boast about than all of them together. You will soon learn why. Here follows a step by step guide that starts in the jungle and ends with a tantalizing piece of chocolate as it approaches you mouth.

1. HARVESTING

We mentioned earlier that the cocoa fruits are attached directly to the trunk of the cocoa tree trunk and branches by means of a short stem. The fruits ripen one after the other throughout the twelve months of the year. It is therefore necessary to harvest and sort the fruit manually. The following example will give you an idea of how much is needed to produce 100 g of chocolate.

Ten fruits yield approximately one kilo of beans, equivalent to 400 g of dried beans, which in turn is what you need to make 500 g of chocolate with a cocoa content of 70 per cent. In other words, you need 20 fruits to make a normal (100 g) size Valrhona or Amadei bar.

2. FERMENTATION

Like many of our favourite foods, cocoa needs to be fermented. The pods are either fermented whole or split. The most common methods are to scoop out the pulp with the seeds inside and either ferment it in a large box or in a pit in the ground lined with banana leaves. In both cases, hundreds of kilos, sometimes as much as a tonne per box or pit, are processed at any one time. The beans are covered in banana leaves and sacking and fermented for 3–6 days. The beans are stirred regularly to ensure that a good supply of oxygen aids fermentation.

Fermentation brings out the characteristic chocolate aromas, kills off the germ inside the seed and separates the bean from the mucilaginous pulp. The beans oxidize at the end of the fermenting process, which is when they acquire their final colour as the centre of the bean goes from white via purple to chocolate brown in a complex process involving alcohol, lactic acid and acetic acid fermentation. The bitterness of the bean is toned down and the typical character of the cocoa becomes fully developed during roasting.

3. DRYING

After fermentation, the water content in the beans quickly needs to be reduced from sixty per cent to seven or eight per cent. This is normally achieved by spreading them out on straw mats and then keep stirring them to expose them to the sun and the wind. This process goes on for a couple of weeks. Producers need to ensure that the temperature does not get too low or the humidity too high in order to prevent mould, and thereby an unpleasant taste, from developing. Apart from sun-drying, beans are desiccated by heating or tumbling. Regardless of method, it is important to avoid that bitter notes form in temperatures above 65–70 °C. After drying, the beans are mechanically burnished and sorted.

4. SORTING

At this 'nursery' stage too, the beans are sorted according to quality. Quality may vary depending on the season and the way the weather has affected the first steps of the process. From a quality point of view, a large, plump bean is better than a small, flat one. After sorting, the beans are packed and kept in a controlled climate to avoid invasive humidity and aromas. The bean sacs are often sprayed with insecticide before and after transport to ensure that no uninvited guests consume the contents.

5. ROASTING

Roasting is normally done on an industrial scale. The first step is the removal of foreign objects. The beans are then usually treated with hot steam at a temperature of between 110 and 150 degrees Celsius depending on bean type. Roasting takes between twenty and fifty minutes. This is when the flavours are honed to perfection and the cocoa aromas in the bean are fully developed. Criollo and Trinitario, with their more subtle aromas, are roasted at lower temperatures and for a shorter period, while more robust beans such as Forastero are roasted longer at higher temperatures. Roasting not only adds aroma and flavour, but serves to eliminate unpleasant, acidic aromas. Low quality beans can be roasted longer to conceal defects. An added advantage is that the shells become brittle and can be mechanically removed.

6. BLENDING, CRUSHING AND GRINDING

Cocoa beans are blended according to quality, origin or type, just like coffee or wine. Once the desired blend has been arrived at, the beans are coarsely crushed into what is known in the business as *grué*. They are then submitted to a second grinding during which the heat produced by the friction causes the now much finer particles and cocoa butter to blend into a liquid, *cocoa liquor*, half of which is cocoa butter.

7. PRESSING

Thanks to an invention made by a Dutchman by the name of van Houten in 1828, the next step involves pressing the cocoa mass in order to separate the cocoa butter from the cocoa solids. Solids and butter are later combined in varying proportions depending on type of end product.

8. CONCHING

In order to make chocolate from the refined raw ingredients – the cocoa butter and solids – sugar, and usually vanilla and lecithin, are added. The lecithin acts as an emulsifier, i.e. it renders the mixture more homogenous. The ingredients are mixed and kneaded together in temperatures that vary between 55 °C and 88 °C. Sugar crystals are ground down, the ingredients blend and unwanted substances, certain acids for example, are eliminated. The word 'conching' derives from a machine invented by Rodolph Lindt in 1879, which resembled a seashell. The French word for seashell is *conche*. The degree of conching varies between manufacturers. Chocolate that is conched for a long period becomes creamier and the end result is better. The conching period goes on for anything between four hours and three days.

9. TEMPERING

Before it is moulded, the chocolate undergoes a process called tempering. It eliminates the risk for the chocolate becoming coarse, grainy and dull-coloured and makes it shiny and hard. It involves heating the chocolate to a temperature just over its melting point, which is 48–50 °C for dark chocolate, and then reducing it to 27–28 °C. It is poured into the mould at 31–32 °C, which is just over melting point. Tempering is necessary in order for the chocolate to loosen from the mould.

'A pound of chocolate a day, a healthy regular diet and plenty of exercise.'

Katherine Hepburn (1907–2003) on how she stayed fit into a very old age.

The History of Chocolate

We learned earlier that the cocoa tree thrives in a considerably warmer and more humid climate than we are normally used to. It gives us some idea of the exotic roots of this highly processed utility plant.

It is of course not entirely clear how it all came about, but it is generally agreed that cocoa has been cultivated for around 3,000 years. According to one theory, cocoa was originally grown in the Orinoco valley of the Amazonas. Our journey in time may go as far back as to the Olmeks, an Indian tribe that may well have been familiar with, and would have known how to process, the delicious cocoa beans as far back as 2000 BC. The Olmeks lived in the southern part of present-day Mexico and Belize, an area with ideal growing conditions. Olmek was an early civilization that preceded the cultures that would later come to flourish in the region, many of which used cocoa for worship, economic transactions and for its healing properties. The Olmek theory is supported by traces of a cocoa industry from around 600 BC near Belize in Central America.

Genetic studies confirm the historically and geographically diverse origins of Criollo and Forastero. Moreover, Criollo beans have been found in several locations in South and Central America.

CONQUERING THE COCOA BEAN
Much later, in the 16th century AD, the Aztecs came to rule after the rise and fall of a number of indigenous cultures. It is a period of South and Central American history we know more about thanks to the exploration undertaken by Columbus and Hernán Cortés' defeat of the sophisticated Aztec empire. Its capital, Tenochtitlan, where Mexico City is now located, was five times larger than 16th century London. The Aztec capital was well organized with white-washed houses placed in a strict grid pattern; a form of town planning that was to emerge in Europe and North America at a much later date in world history.

Both the Aztecs and the earlier pre-Columbian Maya civilization believed that cocoa was a paradise seed given to them by their harvest god, sometimes known as Quetzalcoatl. Cocoa beans were used as currency and, because of their divine origin, as an ingredient in ritual beverages. The health-giving, reviving and aphrodisiac effects contributed to its high status. Cocoa beans were an important ingredient in a drink called xocoatl. The word is a compound made up of the Aztec words for 'bitter' and 'water'. It was made from cocoa beans that were ground into a paste by means of a pestle and mortar. The paste was added to various concoctions that contained, for example, corn flour for texture and spices such as chilli and cinnamon. Red plant juice was sometimes added for colour.

Cocoa was a valuable commodity due to its health-giving effects and divine origins. It was used exclusively by the higher social strata. Only priests and dignitaries enjoyed the privilege of experiencing the

heat, pungency and courage offered by cocoa. Price lists using cocoa beans as a form of currency show how greatly valued the beans were. They quote anything from single beans that would pay for a rabbit to ten beans for a courtesan and as much as ten times that amount for a superior-quality slave. With this in mind, we can establish that the ruler that Hernán Cortés encountered during his conquest in 1519, was one of the richest men in the world, measured in his own currency. The Aztec ruler Montezuma II had about one thousand tonnes of cocoa beans stashed away in the cellars under his palace. Since there are 830–1000 beans to the kilo, Montezuma II could have bought himself a whole army of slaves.

Legend has it that he was also a major consumer of drinking chocolate. When he was at the peak of his power, he consumed about fifty bowls of xocoatl a day.

Christopher Columbus (1451–1506) arrived in Central America less than twenty years before Hernán Cortés laid the several hundred years old Aztec empire in ruins. During his fourth and final voyage, in 1502,

he stepped ashore on the island of Guanaja in present-day Honduras, where he became aware of the fact that the Aztecs bought cocoa beans from the Olmeks. The Olmeks were in decline, but were still dealing in cocoa, pottery, furs and volcanic glass in a major way. Since the climate in the region was unfavourable, the Aztecs did not, as far as we know, cultivate cocoa. Instead, they bought it from the Olmeks whose former domain had become reduced to an area located in present-day south Veracruz and west Tabasco, which is precisely where Hernán Cortés would later land.

Despite the fact that Columbus witnessed the thriving trade in beans, he appreciated neither its appeal nor its value. He made a half-hearted and unsuccessful attempt to introduce this royal crop at the Spanish court. Cocoa would not catch on in Europe until Hernán Cortés finally returned to Spain in 1527.

The Spaniards arrived in Central America at about the same time as the Aztecs expected the return of their feathered god, Quetzalcoatl, who was no other than the gardener in Paradise and the deity that had

given them the cocoa bean. Since there were many similarities between their mythology and the helmets, armour, weapons and other paraphernalia brought by Cortés, their resistance was remarkably weak.

Hernán Cortés and his conquistadors crushed Montezuma II, and after the defeat of Tenochtitlan in 1521, the Aztec empire lay in ruins. Cortés was appointed governor of New Spain by the king of old Spain, Charles V. Cortés had entertained plans for introducing cocoa at the Spanish court early on, but he would not succeed until he finally returned to Spain for good. And it did not become universal until much later.

THE BREAKTHROUGH

It took a long time before chocolate started to gain in popularity. During the colonial culture that developed after the Spanish conquests, many of the Meso-American traditions continued. One was the use of drinking chocolate. As merchant ships started to ply the route between Spain and New Spain in 1580, products and mores – drinking chocolate for example – were introduced to the old world. It was adapted to European tastes, and ingredients such as sugar, vanilla and milk were added. The court of Philip II took to drinking chocolate, and the custom spread to other privileged parts of society across Europe. Drinking chocolate was enjoyed in Spanish monasteries as early as in the 1530s and -40s, for example, and in 1569, Pope Pius V allowed drinking chocolate to be consumed during lent. Chocolate was introduced in the Italian city of Florence in 1606 and the British established their first cocoa plantation in Jamaica in 1656.

▲ Production line at a factory established in Malmö, Sweden, by the Swiss Cloetta brothers in 1873.

'The superiority of chocolate, both for health and nourishment, will soon give it the same preference over tea and coffee in America which it has in Spain.'

Thomas Jefferson

It took many years before cocoa and chocolate became more widely available. It was an expensive, imported commodity, and with limited availability followed a high price tag. One step on the way to increased availability was when chocolate production and semi-manufactured cocoa products were mentioned in newspapers and in general conversation in the early 18th century; industrial manufacture of chocolate started in France and Spain at the end of the 1700s. Industrialization in general benefited chocolate manufacturers through the introduction of mechanized grinding and blending. A major step was taken in 1828, when the Dutchman Coenraad van Houten invented a press that separated the cocoa butter from the solids. This was the dawn of modern chocolate making. It now became possible to make harder chocolate, and by removing the solids, white chocolate. The first attempts at making pralines that were made in Switzerland at the start of the 1820s were imitated elsewhere, chocolate bars became more widely available and the first moulded chocolate bar was launched in England in 1847. It was marketed as 'the edible chocolate bar'.

Further improvement arrived when Henri Nestlé invented condensed milk in 1875. Also in 1875, Swiss chocolatier Daniel Peter was able to market the first hard milk chocolate bar, which he made by adding condensed milk to his original recipe. Quality improved considerably four years later when another Swiss chocolate manufacturer, Rodolphe Lindt, found that a more homogenous and better tasting product could be achieved by extensive kneading of the chocolate mass at various temperatures. It has the not insignificant effect of allowing the chocolate to melt deliciously in the mouth. This was the invention of the so-called conching method.

At the end of the 19th century, a Frenchman by the name of Dubuisson developed even more rational methods for roasting and grinding cocoa beans. It was at this time that production got underway at several of the manufacturers whose brands have survived even to this day: Nestlé, Toblerone, Lindt, Cloetta and Mazetti, Marabou and Valrhona.

The praline was the original chocolate product, invented at a time when chocolate manufacture rather resembled cake-making. With the advent of water and steam power and industrialization in general, it became possible to modernize the processing of raw materials and end products. Cocoa became more widely available, and chocolate was consumed by all strata of society, but the marketing of chocolate is a fairly recent development. A hundred years ago and up until some twenty years ago, chocolate was marketed in the same way as confectionary, with images of elegant ladies enjoying the luxury of pralines. In the last twenty years it is more about mass production of sweets and of gourmet products made from high-quality ingredients.

Two examples of the way in which sophisticated products with high cocoa content are marketed today are Valrhona, who came out with their 70 % cocoa in 1984, and Amedei, who came on the market in 1990.

This sums up the history of chocolate so far. Chocolate has gone from being an exclusive, regal or sacred luxury item to something that can be enjoyed every day by everyone. These days, the choice of chocolate products is vast and impressive. In the spirit of the Aztecs, chocolate can be luxurious and exclusive with an almost religious effect on those who have already been converted to its joys.

SOME IMPORTANT DATES

600 BC – Cocoa trees are cultivated in what is now Belize in Central America.

AD 1500 – The Aztec empire reaches its climax during the reign of Montezuma II. The cocoa bean is of religious and economic importance.

1502 – Christopher Columbus lands on the island of Guanaja. As far as we know, he was the first European to learn about cocoa.

1519 – Hernán Cortés lands on the Tabasco coast. Within two years, he has conquered the Aztecs.

1527 – Hernán Cortés brings cocoa on his final journey back east.

1580s – The first merchant ships begin to sail between New Spain and Europe. Cocoa beans are one of the products on board.

1659 – The British begin to establish cocoa plantations in Jamaica.

1737 – Carolus Linnaeus names the cocoa tree Theobroma cacao.

1824 – John Cadbury begins selling drinking chocolate at Bull Street in Birmingham, England.

1828 – In July, Coenraad van Houten receives the patent for his hydraulic cocoa press.

1847 – The first moulded chocolate bar is launched in England by Fry & Sons.

1875 – Daniel Peter is able to market milk chocolate thanks to condensed milk, an invention by Henri Nestlé.

1879 – Rodolphe Lindt invents the conching method, thereby giving birth to the modern chocolate bar.

1924 – Valrhona is established at Tournon, France.

1940 – During the war, the American firm Hershey launches a chocolate that can withstand tropical temperatures by exchanging cocoa butter for vegetable fat that melts at a higher temperature.

1984 – Valrhona are first to produce chocolate with 70 % cocoa content.

1990 – Italian Amedei set up business.

The Beneficial Effects of Chocolate

The beneficial effects of chocolate were discovered already by the Maya. Cocoa was used as an aphrodisiac, and ritual intercourse was performed to the honour of the cocoa god Chac Ek-Chuah.

Cocoa was later noted for its general health-giving properties. The first scientific treatise on chocolate was published in 1631 by a physician, Colmonero de Ledesma. There have, on the other hand, been discussions as to whether the stimulating properties and caffeine-like effects of theobromine can be addictive. In 1705, Frenchman Daniel Duncan was concerned about the abuse of cocoa as well as of coffee and tea, and the beneficial effects of cocoa have been debated ever since.

Cocoa beans are in fact rich in minerals (iron, zinc, potassium, magnesium) and vitamins (B and E) as well as fluoride and phosphates. They also contain caffeine and the caffeine-like substance theobromine, which also has a stimulating effect.

Cocoa butter is stable on account of the high antioxidant content, the beneficial effects of which we are informed on an almost daily basis in various health magazines. Polyphenols are among the most valuable, and these are of course present in cocoa. They are important because they prevent the oxidation and storing of cholesterol in the vascular system, and some say it slows down the aging process. Scientific journals such as the Lancet and the British Medical Journal have commented on the positive effects of chocolate in preventing the common cold.

Less scientific publications too occasionally publish articles on the role of compounds known as flavonoids, which are found in chocolate, in preventing cardio-vascular disease. Cocoa also contains blood-thinning substances, tyramine for example, which may cause the blood vessels to dilate and potentially contributes to lowering blood pressure; an undesirable effect for migraine sufferers. Chocolate is frequently blamed for causing this debilitating disorder caused by blood vessels in the brain becoming dilated.

Against this background, it is no wonder Linnaeus named the cocoa tree Theobroma cacao, or food for the gods. Anyone eating a lot of chocolate may even reach a state of euphoria. This has previously been attributed to the amphetamine-like substance phenyl ethylamine, which is the same substance that causes people to fall in love. But you need to eat around fifteen kilos of chocolate for the feeling to kick in. The euphoria is instead explained by the fact that cocoa releases anandamide, a substance that is vaguely similar to THC, the active substance in cannabis, which may have been the source of the notion that chocolate is an aphrodisiac. Both Montezuma II and the womanizer Casanova are reported to have drunk some fifty cups of chocolate a day. It probably gave them the energy to deal with one thing or another ...

Accompaniments

As you will see from the rest of this book, there is a virtually unlimited number of ways you can use chocolate.

Before we get to the recipe section, we will offer some general advice on traditional and unexpected flavour combinations involving chocolate. We will also be offering a few tips on what you need to think about in order to get out as much as possible from the unlimited range of taste sensations offered by chocolate.

THE BASICS

Just like any other well-chosen ingredient or accompaniment, chocolate can bring out aromas and flavours in drinks or food. Here are some tips worth remembering:

Cocoa content. Chocolate with high cocoa content tends to be bitter-tasting and is therefore unsuitable for matching with other bitter-tasting beverages or foods.

Strength and complexity means that the beverage that accompanies a chocolate dessert must be richer and more full-bodied than the dessert itself.

The drink must be sweeter than the dessert, or it will be perceived as unpleasantly dry.

CLASSICS AND COMBINATIONS

Chocolate cake and stout – A favourite that may sound a little unexpected, but that has become rather common, is to serve chocolate cake and lightly whipped cream with a very sweet stout, or Baltic porter, a version of stout that is brewed in Finland, Estonia, Latvia, Lithuania, Poland, Russia, Ukraine, Denmark and Sweden.

White chocolate, sweet wine and bourbon – The soft vanilla tone present in white chocolate goes extremely well with sweet and fruity wines such as Muscat, sweet Riesling and wines made from Semillon grapes. Bourbon is another excellent companion, especially to white chocolate and butterscotch or caramel combinations. The whiskey character marries well with vanilla, caramel and milky chocolate tones. One more surprisingly successful combination is white chocolate and a good Belgian cherry beer, Timmermans Kriek Tradition, for example.

Milk chocolate and Tokay – White chocolate can normally be substituted by milk chocolate, and a bourbon to go with it is never wrong since milk chocolate often has a butterscotch note that is emphasized in combination with the burnt sugar notes also present in Tokay wine. Milk chocolate also combines well with sweet dessert wines like Madeira, Commandaria St John from Cyprus or wines made from gewürztraminer grapes.

Dark chocolate – Chocolate with high cocoa content does not combine well with anything that has been aged in oak barrels. You also need to keep in mind that high cocoa content brings out the alcohol flavour. Fruity dark chocolate from, for example, Papua New Guinea or Madagascar go well with rich, fruity dessert wines like,

WHAT IS CHOCOLATE MADE OF?

The basic ingredients are **cocoa powder** and **cocoa butter**. Fine chocolate also contains sugar, vanilla or vanillin and lecithin.

The **sugar** may either be of the sweetest kind, that is to say plain white, refined sugar, or it may be more full-bodied, caramel-like raw sugar or unrefined cane sugars such as Muscovado. Some types of chocolate, low-calorie or diet products for example, are sweetened with honey, fructose or saccharin.

Lecithin in chocolate helps the homogeneous mixing of the ingredients. Organic chocolate is made without lecithin since it is normally made from soy beans and it is hard to determine whether they have been organically grown.

The **vanilla** or **vanillin** content marks the difference between a more expensive and a cheaper product. The more expensive brands use real vanilla that offers more subtle flavour combinations than the industrially manufactured vanillin. Some compromise by using vanilla extract, which is made from vanilla-flavoured sugar. According to current legislation, vanilla extract must contain a minimum of 15 milligrams of vanilla per 100 grams of sugar.

Milk, is added in the form of powdered milk with varying milk fat content and character depending on the method used for removing the water.

for instance, a red Moscatel or young, full-bodied wines such as Banyuls and LBV Port. Like matches like when it comes to food and drink, so a nutty, burned chocolate from Ghana or the West Indies should be accompanied by a beverage with a distinct burned note. Commandaria St John or Madeira is another suggestion, and why not try an old Pedro Ximenez sherry – an explosion of nutty caramel flavours.

More tips. Grenadine's chocolate guru Maja Berthas calls for greater creativity. Be bold! She recommends dry sherry with chocolate cream. Why not give it a try? You need to combine it with a piece of toast with a little olive oil and sea salt to balance the flavours, but it is divine! If this whets your appetite, do not hesitate to mix dark chocolate with tapenade, or put a few pieces of 85 % chocolate in your chilli-con-carne.

Good luck! The worst that can happen is that your food gets more interesting, but perhaps not very nice. On the other hand, when your get it right it can be magic, delectably delicious!

'Chemically speaking, chocolate really is the world's perfect food.'

Michael Levine, nutrition researcher

OUR FAVOURITE RECIPES

Chocolate Cream
with raspberries & chilli

4–6 servings

INGREDIENTS

300 ml double cream

300 g dark chocolate

1 egg yolk

1 ½ tbsp butter

2 tsp vanilla-flavoured icing sugar

1 pinch chilli powder or a little fresh chilli

10–15 fresh raspberries

Topping:

Fresh raspberries

100 g fine dark chocolate (preferably chilli-flavoured) for making chocolate shavings

Fresh red chillies if you dare

1. Mash the raspberries to a pulp.

2. Heat the cream slowly and simmer for about a minute. Remove from the heat.

3. Break up the chocolate and mix the pieces with the cream. Stir until the chocolate has melted. Keep stirring vigorously, adding the egg yolk. Add the butter, raspberry pulp, chilli and vanilla-flavoured icing sugar. Keep stirring until smooth.

4. Pour into 4–6 odd glasses. Cool for about one hour.

5. Make chocolate shavings for the topping using a potato peeler.

Serve with chocolate shavings, a few raspberries and chillies for the bold!

Raspberries are virtual health bombs, choc-full of manganese, vitamin C and fibre. Best of all is that they contain large amounts of an unusual type of beneficial antioxidants that have not been found in any other food in the world.

Chocolate Truffle Cake

6–8 slices

INGREDIENTS

250 g fine dark chocolate, minimum 50 %

125 g unsalted butter

500 ml double cream

4 egg whites

4 egg yolks

150 g sugar

2 tbsp cocoa powder

Topping

100 g grated dark chocolate

Fresh raspberries

Vanilla-flavoured icing sugar

1. **Preparation:** Place a baking parchment at the bottom of a loose-bottomed tin, approx. 20 cm, and sprinkle a little cocoa powder over it (optional). Butter the sides.

2. Melt the chocolate, butter and cream in a heat-proof bowl suspended over boiling water. Leave to cool for five minutes. Preheat the oven to 180 °C (gas mark 4).

3. Whip the egg yolks and 100 g of the sugar until fluffy. Stir into the chocolate mixture.

4. Whisk the egg white until stiff. Whisk in the rest of the sugar. Fold into the egg mixture. Add cocoa powder and stir until smooth.

5. Pour the mixture into the tin and bake for approx. 35 minutes. Cool in the tin for ten minutes, then transfer the cake to a plate.

6. Top with grated chocolate and a little vanilla-flavoured icing sugar.

Serve with fresh raspberries.

In the 17th century, cocoa was a typically Spanish phenomenon, and even though the Spanish-born French queen, Maria Theresa, adored chocolate, cocoa did not become popular in France until the French acquired their own plantations in Martinique and it became 'an act of patriotism' to buy colonial products. Chocolate gained in popularity, in some places it even overtook coffee.

Espresso Mousse

4–6 servings

INGREDIENTS

150 g dark chocolate, and a little extra for garnish

250 ml double cream

1 egg yolk

50 g granulated sugar

1–2 tbsp espresso powder or 3–4 tbsp extra strong espresso

TIP!

Add a little brandy, orange liqueur or almond liqueur.

1. Melt the chocolate in a heat-proof bowl suspended over boiling water or in a microwave oven together with 50 ml of the cream. Whip the remaining cream lightly. Stir a quarter of the whipped cream into the chocolate.

2. Whisk together egg yolks and sugar in a large bowl. Stir in the coffee.

3. Pour the chocolate mixture into the egg mixture and gently fold in the rest of the cream.

4. Pour into individual cups and chill for approx. 2 hours until set.

There is some argument as to the origin of the word 'espresso'. Some claim it has to do with the fact that the coffee is made under pressure, but the most likely explanation is that it derives from the Italian word for 'quick'. In Italy, you simply order a *caffè*.

White Chocolate Parfait

with raspberries and blackberries

4–6 servings

INGREDIENTS

200 ml double cream

200 g white chocolate

3 egg whites

100 g sugar

3 tbsp raspberry liqueur

3 tbsp blackberry liqueur

Garnish with fresh raspberries and blackberries

TIP!

Replace the liqueur with fresh berries for an alcohol-free version.

1. Slowly melt the chocolate and cream. Stir until the chocolate has melted completely. Remove from the heat and leave to cool.

2. Whisk in the sugar, a little at a time, until the mixture becomes thick and smooth. Add the chocolate/cream mixture and the liqueur and stir a couple of times.

3. Pour into four individual bowls. Freeze for 3 hours or overnight.

4. Remove from the freezer and top with fresh raspberries and blackberries. Leave in the bowls or turn out on a plate.

White chocolate is chocolate too, despite rumours to the contrary. White chocolate is made from cocoa butter. The characteristic spicy cocoa flavour, and the brown colour, comes from the cocoa solids. White chocolate has a virtually neutral flavour and aroma, so vanilla is often added.

Ice Choco Latte

4 servings

INGREDIENTS

250 ml strong coffee or espresso

250 ml milk

75 g dark chocolate

5–10 ice cubes (for cooling)

1 scoop vanilla ice cream

Topping:

2 tbsp lightly whipped cream

1 tsp grated chocolate

TIP!

Flavour your ice choco latte with some good spirits, preferably rum or whisky! The choco latte can be served warm (skip the ice), but remember to use heat-proof glasses.

1. Melt the chocolate in a heat-proof bowl suspended over boiling water or in a microwave oven.

2. Mix warm coffee and chocolate and set aside to cool.

3. Pour cold chocolate coffee, cold milk, ice cream and ice into a blender and blend until the ice is completely crushed (add more ice for a more 'frozen' consistency). Alternatively, mix all the ingredients in a cup, stir with a long spoon and serve without ice.

4. Top with whipped cream and grated chocolate.

The word 'coffee' comes from *gawah*, originally Arabic for 'wine'. When Muslims were no longer permitted to drink alcohol and had to find an alternative, the beverage that took its place was called the same.

Crème Brûlée
made with white chocolate

4–6 servings

INGREDIENTS

1 vanilla pod

5 egg yolks

150 g sugar

500 ml double cream

125 g white chocolate

TIP!
Serve the crème brûlée with or without fresh berries.

1. **Preparation**: Preheat the oven to 130 °C (gas mark 1) and take out some 100–150 ml ovenproof dessert bowls. Slit the vanilla pod down the middle and scrape the seeds into a saucepan and add the rest of the pod. Gently melt the chocolate together with the cream in a small saucepan. Give the mixture a stir every now and then. Take out the vanilla pod and remove from the heat when the mixture has become completely smooth. Set aside.

2. Beat the egg yolks and 100 g of sugar in a large bowl. Add the vanilla extract and chocolate mixture and mix well.

3. Pour the mixture into the serving bowls. Then put the bowls in a heat-proof dish filled with hot water in the oven and cook until just set, approx. 35–40 minutes.

4. Remove the water-filled dish from the oven and lift out the bowls. Leave to cool for 30 minutes and refrigerate for a few hours or overnight.

5. **Presentation**: Sprinkle the remaining sugar over each bowl and scorch the surface with a small blowtorch or put them as close as possible to the oven grill preheated to 250 °C (gas mark 9) until the sugar turns brittle (but not burnt!).

Serve immediately.

Crème brûlée is a French dessert that is related to the traditional Spanish dessert Crema Catalan, but should not be confused with crème caramel. Crème brûlée is French for 'burned cream'.

Classic Chocolate Truffles

Makes 30–40

INGREDIENTS

150 ml double cream

300 g dark chocolate, approx. 50%

100 g unsalted butter, at room temperature

2 tbsp liqueur or other aromatic spirit, e.g. cognac

Cocoa powder

TIP!

Add your favourite flavourings: chilli, coconut, nougat, chopped nuts, grated orange peel saffron, spice mixture, cinnamon, cardamom, sea salt, coffee powder, a few drops of peppermint oil, or why not something more adult such as rum, whisky, brandy, tequila, grappa, Baileys, Grand Marnier or Cointreau ... experiment!

Truffle mixture:

1. Slowly bring the cream to the boil and remove from the heat. Add chocolate and butter, and keep stirring with a wooden spoon until everything has melted.

2. Transfer the mixture to a bowl. Add the spirits or other flavouring and mix until smooth. Refrigerate for 1–2 hours until the mixture can be handled.

Making the truffles:

3. Pour some cocoa powder on a plate. Roll out truffle-size balls and turn them over in the cocoa powder. For a classic, irregular shape – roll them swiftly or not at all. You can also make balls, cubes, triangles, hearts, stars or, why not, little miniature bottles? Use your imagination!

Alternatively, dip the truffles in some fine melted chocolate, but leave out at room temperature before serving. Truffles keep for about 2–3 days in the refrigerator.

The most common use for chocolate truffles is in pralines, where they are spiked with, for example, spices, liquors, mint oil or coffee. The name refers to the traditional lumps that resemble the truffle fungus.

Spicy Chilli Chocolate Muffins

Makes 12

INGREDIENTS

250 g wheat flour

1 tsp bicarbonate of soda

4 tbsp cocoa powder

100 g butter, at room temperature

2 eggs

150 g sugar

125 g brown sugar

150 ml crème fraîche

5 tbsp milk

1 fresh, finely chopped, red chilli or ½ –1 tsp chilli (beware, it is hot)

300 g dark chocolate, chopped

Icing:

100 g dark chocolate

2 tbsp unsalted butter

2 tbsp cream

1 fresh chilli for garnish – if you dare!

1. **Preparation:** Preheat the oven to 190 °C (gas mark 5). Take a 12 muffin tin and line with paper muffin cups. Crush the chocolate with a pestle and mortar, chop or place in a plastic bag and beat with a hammer or rolling pin.

2. Mix flour, bicarbonate of soda, cocoa powder and chilli in a bowl. Add butter and mix Beat eggs, caster sugar and brown sugar until fluffy. Add the crème fraîche, milk and the flour mixture. Mix well and stir in the crushed chocolate.

3. Pour the mixture into the paper cups and top with chocolate chips. Bake at the centre of the oven for 25–30 minutes.

4. Leave to cool for 10 minutes in the tin, transfer to a wire cooling rack and leave to cool completely.

Icing:
Slowly melt chocolate, cream and butter.
Spread the icing on top of the muffins.

Garnish with fresh chillies.

Chilli has been cultivated for at least 8,000 years, and is said to help against everything from cancer to salmonella. Red chilli is rich in vitamin C and beta-carotene. All types of chilli contain B-vitamins, potassium and magnesium, which is good for the blood pressure.

White, Light and Dark
Chocolate Pannacotta

3 x 4 mini pannacottas

INGREDIENTS

1 vanilla pod

3 gelatine leaves

250 ml double cream

125 ml milk

40 g white chocolate

40 g milk chocolate

40 g dark chocolate

2 tbsp sugar

TIP!
Invite your friends for a pannacotta testing!

1. Soak the gelatine leaves in cold water for 5 minutes.

2. Slit the vanilla pod down the middle and scrape the seeds into a saucepan, add the rest of the pod. Bring the cream, milk and sugar to the boil and immediately remove from the heat.

3. Squeeze the gelatine leaves to get rid of most of the water, add them to the saucepan and dissolve over low heat.

4. Distribute the mixture between 3 small saucepans, adding the white chocolate to the first, the light to the next and the dark to the third. Stir with a wooden spoon to make sure that the chocolate has melted completely. Remove from the heat.

5. Take out 12 small dessert glasses (e.g. heat-proof shots glasses), preferably with a stem. Pour a few drops of liquid chocolate on the bottom of each glass for a more festive look (white, light and dark). Pour the pannacotta slowly on top of the chocolate.

6. Leave to cool for a few minutes, then refrigerate for at least 2 hours.

Serve with fresh berries and dust with vanilla-flavoured icing sugar. If you would rather not serve the pannacotta in the glasses, you can dip the bottom of the glass in hot water and then loosen the pannacotta by running a sharp knife around the rim. Turn out on a plate.

Pannacotta is Italian for 'cooked cream', but nobody knows when, where and how this dessert was created. It may have been in the mountain regions of northern Italy, famous for producing cream, which was eaten with fruits and nuts. Some early recipes included the boiling of fish bones for the gelatine effect. There was no added sugar, however, as it was an expensive commodity. Variations of this dessert can be found in Greece and France.

Rum Chocolate Cake

6–8 slices

INGREDIENTS

Sponge:

90 g wheat flour

50 g cocoa powder

1 tsp baking powder

250 g dark chocolate

50 ml water

175 g unsalted butter, at room temperature

300 g Muscovado sugar

4 eggs

100 ground almonds

Chocolate cream:

200 g dark chocolate, 70 %

200 ml cream

4–6 tbsp dark, old rum

Glaze:

150 g dark chocolate, 70 %

3 tbsp unsalted butter

1 dash dark, old rum

Garnish:

Sprig of mint

Raspberries

Grated chocolate

Sponge:

1. **Preparation:** Preheat the oven to 160 ℃ (gas mark 3). Butter a round, 20 cm tin. Mix flour, cocoa powder and baking powder in a small bowl. Melt the chocolate slowly in a heat-proof bowl suspended over boiling water, stir a few times and then add the water.

2. Stir together butter and sugar in a large bowl. Beat in the eggs. Mix in the melted chocolate.

3. Add the flour mixture a little at a time and then the almonds.

4. Pour the mixture into the tin and bake until the cake has risen, approx. one hour. It should still be a little sticky in the middle. Allow the cake to cool before you remove the tin.

5. Choose a good, sharp knife to cut the sponge into three separate layers.

Chocolate cream:

6. Slowly heat butter, cream, rum and dark chocolate in a saucepan. Set aside and cool at room temperature. The end result should resemble thick cream.

7. Transfer the cake to a plate and spread chocolate cream between the two bottom layers.

Icing:

8. Melt the chocolate either in a heat-proof bowl suspended over boiling water or in a microwave oven, add the rum and mix until smooth. Pour the icing over the cake (either after it has been cut into slices or over the whole cake).

Serve with fresh berries, mint and grated chocolate.

Rum is in a Caribbean spirit made from sugar cane. Dark rum should acquire its colour from aging, but artificial colouring is used for cheaper brands.

Dark Chocolate Fondant

4–6 servings

INGREDIENTS

200 g fine, dark chocolate, 50 %

100 g butter

4 eggs

150 g brown sugar

50 g flour

Pinch of salt

Fresh raspberries for garnish

1. **Preparation:** Preheat the oven to 180 °C (gas mark 4). Butter some ovenproof dessert bowls and sprinkle with a little flour. Melt the chocolate and butter slowly in a heat-proof bowl suspended over boiling water on the stove.

2. Meanwhile: Beat eggs and sugar in a large bowl until fluffy. Add the flour.

3. Mix in the salt and melted chocolate mixture. Stir.

4. Divide the mixture evenly between the ovenproof bowls and bake in the oven for 10–12 minutes, depending on the oven. Leave to cool for a few minutes.

Garnish with a few raspberries.

Chocolate is an energy-rich and healthy food, at least that is how the US Army has looked at it since the Second World War. However, the Gulf War in 1990 confronted them with a major problem. The chocolate bars would soon melt in the heat. How did they solve the problem? The struck up a collaboration with chocolate manufacturer Hershey and invented a chocolate bar that can withstand up to 60 °C without melting!

Chocolate Ice Cream

4–6 servings

INGREDIENTS

400 ml milk

400 ml cream

50 g bitter cocoa powder

200 g dark chocolate, 60–70 %

5 egg yolks

100 g sugar

TIP!

The flavours will develop if you cover the ice cream and refrigerate it overnight. Why not make several batches with different types of chocolate, nuts and berries and ask your guests to choose their favourite?

Do not go for the cheapest you can find, choose a clean-tasting, fine chocolate you like from a specialist outlet.

1. Bring the milk and cream to the boil. Remove the saucepan from the heat and whisk in the cocoa powder. Break up the chocolate and add the pieces.

2. Melt the chocolate slowly while stirring with a wooden spoon. Replace the saucepan over a low flame if the chocolate does not melt completely.

3. Beat eggs and sugar until fluffy and stir the mixture into the chocolate.

4. Simmer slowly for 10 minutes, stirring all the time until thick.

5. Remove from the heat and leave to cool. Refrigerate for 2–3 hours before pouring the mixture into an ice-cream maker. Run until the ice-cream has set or until the blade stops. Scoop the ice-cream into a plastic container and freeze.

Serve the freshly made ice-cream with strong coffee or a fine brandy.

Ice-cream has been known since around 60 BC, when the Roman emperor Nero ordered ice to be fetched down from the mountains and mixed with fruits. In the 13th century, Marco Polo introduced a method for making ice and milk mixtures that he had learned in China.

Chocolate Almond Dreams

Makes 20

INGREDIENTS

175 g unsalted butter

100 g extra fine sugar

1 egg yolk

200 g ground almonds

150 g wheat flour

100 g dark chocolate

Icing:

150 g white chocolate, chopped

2 tbsp brandy

TIP!

Vary with three different glazes – white chocolate, milk chocolate and dark chocolate.

1. Line three trays with baking parchment.

2. Mix butter and sugar until white and fluffy. Beat together egg yolk, flour and almonds. Wrap the dough in cling film and refrigerate for approx. 1.5–2 hours.

3. Preheat the oven to 160 °C (gas mark 3). Roll the mixture into 40 small balls. Place the balls sparsely on the trays.

4. Bake until golden, approx. 20–25 minutes. Transfer the parchment with the cookies to a wire cooling rack and leave to cool.

5. Melt the chocolate in a heat-proof bowl suspended over boiling water. Remove the baking parchment and spread melted chocolate on the flat end of each cookie.

6. Join two cookies, flat ends together, and put them back on the baking parchment and leave until set.

Icing:

Melt the chocolate and add the brandy. Dip one half of each double cookie into the icing. Leave to set on the baking parchment.

Hooray! Regardless of what the school dentist may have told you, the tannin in chocolate prevents caries! Moreover, the cocoa butter prevents the sugar from sticking to your teeth, and chocolate contains both calcium and fluoride.

Chocolate Droplets
with toasted almonds

Makes 16–20

INGREDIENTS

200 g of your favourite dark or milk chocolate

300 g toasted almond flakes

TIP!

These chocolate droplets make great Christmas candy, they are quick and easy to adapt to the occasion. Suitable even for the most inveterate non-bakers.

1. Put the toasted almond flakes in a bowl. Melt the chocolate slowly in a heat-proof bowl suspended over boiling water and pour it over the almond flakes. Leave to cool for a few minutes. Meanwhile: line a biscuit sheet with a baking parchment.

2. Spoon the chocolate/almond mixture on the sheet and refrigerate for approx. 30 minutes until set.

Almonds are related to plums, and the part we eat is the seed.
The word almond originates from the Latin *amanda*, meaning 'loveable'.

Hot Lumumba

4–6 servings

INGREDIENTS

1 vanilla pod

600 ml standard milk

100 g dark chocolate, chopped

160 ml dark, old rum

100 ml double cream

Chocolate shavings for garnish

TIP!

Also excellent cold with ice cubes served in a tall glass.

1. Slit the vanilla pod and scrape the seeds into a saucepan, then add the rest of the pod.

2. Pour in the milk, add the chocolate and heat. Stir with a wooden spoon over low heat until the chocolate has melted. Bring almost to the boil. Take out the vanilla pod and set aside.

3. Add the rum.

4. Whip the cream lightly and pour it carefully into the glass.

Serve in a heatproof glass with chocolate shavings.

Lumumba is a long drink named for the Congolese politician Patrice Lumumba.

Sabayon
with Armagnac and dark chocolate

4–6 servings

INGREDIENTS

8 egg yolks

60 g icing sugar

4–6 tbsp Armagnac

1 knob of butter, at room temperature

Garnish:

100 g dark chocolate, min. 50 %

TIP!

This elegant dessert should be served hot or warm. As it cools down, it loses its flavour.

1. **Preparation:** Take a dark chocolate bar (left out at room temperature) and use a potato peeler to make chocolate twists. Refrigerate while you make the sabayon to prevent them from melting when you serve them on top of the warm sabayon.

2. Pour egg yolks, icing sugar and Armagnac into a heat-proof bowl and warm suspended over boiling water. Beat with an electric whisk until thick and fluffy, approx. 15 minutes.

3. Remove the bowl from the water, add butter and continue to whisk for another 12 minutes.

4. Pour the sabayon into dessert glasses.

Top with the previously prepared chocolate shavings from the fridge. Serve with fresh berries and garnish with edible flowers.

Armagnac is made from distilled grapes (a distillate of white wine) from the Armagnac district in the south of France. The difference between Armagnac and its better known relative, Cognac, is that Armagnac is normally only distilled once (these days a two-step distillation process is common), and the fact that Armagnac is thicker and sweeter on account of the grapes growing further south than the grapes from which Cognac, which is lighter, is made.

Kahlúa Chocolate Brownies

with Baileys-vodka chocolate icing

Makes 8–10

INGREDIENTS

115 g unsalted butter

115 g dark chocolate

275 g extra fine sugar

A pinch of salt

2 tsp vanilla-flavoured icing sugar

2 eggs

150 g wheat flour

4 tbsp cocoa powder

150 g dark chocolate (minimum 50 %) broken into pieces

4–6 tbsp Kahlúa

Baileys-vodka chocolate icing:

4 tbsp butter

200 g dark chocolate

4 tbsp Baileys

2 tbsp vodka

The brownie:

1. **Preparation:** Preheat the oven to 190 °C (gas mark 5). Line a large, square brownie tin, ca. 18 x 18 with a baking parchment. Melt the dark chocolate in a heat-proof bowl suspended over boiling water or in a microwave oven.

2. Mix the sugar, salt and vanilla-flavoured icing sugar in a large bowl. Stir in the melted chocolate and Kahlúa. Add the eggs, one at a time, and mix until smooth.

3. Whisk in the flour and cocoa powder. Mix well and pour the batter into the tin.

4. Bake for 35–40 minutes until the centre is dry. Leave to cool.

Icing:

5. Melt the chocolate either in a heat-proof bowl suspended over boiling water or in a microwave oven, add the liqueur and vodka and stir until smooth.

6. Spread the icing over the brownie (either after it has been cut into squares or over the whole cake). Leave until set.

Cut into squares and serve with chocolate shapes.

It you prefer you can replace the alcohol with coffee powder and toffee.

Kahlúa is a rum-based Mexican liqueur flavoured with coffee, herbs and vanilla.

Hazelnut Brownies

Makes 8–10

INGREDIENTS

125 g unsalted butter

200 g dark chocolate, minimum 50 %

4 eggs

250 g sugar

2 tsp vanilla-flavoured icing sugar

125 g wheat flour

1 tsp baking powder

½ tsp salt

100 g chopped hazelnuts

1. **Preparation:** Preheat the oven to 190 ℃ (gas mark 5). Line a large, square brownie tin, ca. 18 x 18 with a baking parchment. Melt the dark chocolate in a heat-proof bowl suspended over boiling water or in a microwave oven.

2. Mix the sugar, salt and vanilla-flavoured icing sugar in a large bowl. Add the melted chocolate and stir. Add the eggs, one at a time, and stir until smooth.

3. Whisk in flour and half of the hazelnuts. Mix well, then pour the batter into the tin.

4. Sprinkle the remaining chopped hazelnuts on top.

5. Bake for 25–30 minutes until dry at the centre. Leave to cool a little before cutting into squares.

Brownies were served in public for the first time at the Chicago Columbian Exposition in 1893. A chef from the local Palmer House Hotel invented it when he was asked by business woman Bertha Palmer to make a dessert for the attending ladies: it had to be 'smaller than a piece of cake and easy to eat out of a lunch box'. The original brownie was covered in apricot icing and included walnuts. They are still made at the hotel according to the original recipe.

Chocolate and Vanilla Delights

4–6 servings

INGREDIENTS

500 ml double cream

60 g extra fine sugar

1 vanilla pod

200 ml crème fraîche

2 tsp gelatine powder

3 tbsp water

50 g dark chocolate

Chocolate shavings

1. Slit the vanilla pod down the middle and scrape the seeds into a saucepan. Add the remains of the pod.

2. Slowly heat the cream, sugar and vanilla. Stir until the sugar has dissolved. Bring to the boil and simmer for 2–3 minutes.

3. Remove the saucepan from the heat and take out the vanilla pod. Stir in the crème fraîche. Transfer the mixture to a large bowl.

4. Pour the water into a small, heat-proof bowl, sprinkle the gelatine powder over the top and leave to soak. Place the bowl over boiling water and stir until the gelatine has dissolved. Then stir into the cream mixture. Transfer one half of the batter to another bowl.

5. Melt the chocolate in a heat-proof bowl suspended over boiling water or in a microwave. Then mix it into one of the bowls of cream. Pour the mixture into dessert glasses and refrigerate until set for 15–20 minutes.

6. Remove the dessert glasses from the fridge and spoon the vanilla mixture on top of the chocolate cream. Return to the fridge and wait for the vanilla cream to set. Garnish with chocolate shavings and fresh berries.

Vanilla is extracted from a type of orchid that grows in tropical and subtropical climates. After the orchid has wilted, it grows a seed pod that does not taste of vanilla at all. The aroma does not develop until the pods are steeped in boiling water and fermented in the sun for several months.

Chocolate Chip Cookies

Makes 16–20

INGREDIENTS

100 g dark chocolate, 70 %

125 g flour

50 g ground almonds

1 pinch of salt

100 g butter at room temperature

1 egg

60 g icing sugar

2 tsp vanilla-flavoured icing sugar

3–4 tbsp cocoa powder

1. **Preparation:** Mix together the flour, almonds and salt in a bowl and set aside. Chop the chocolate into suitable chocolate-chip-cookie-size pieces.

2. Mix plain icing sugar, vanilla-flavoured icing sugar and butter. Add the egg and mix well.

3. Divide the batter between two bowls and add the cocoa powder to one of them, mix well.

4. Divide the flour mixture between the two bowls and stir until smooth. Leave for 30 minutes.

5. Preheat the oven to 180 ºC (gas mark 4) and line a biscuit sheet with baking parchment. Roll out ten balls from the each dough. Put them out on the tray and flatten. Press a few chocolate chips into each cookie. Bake for 8 minutes. Remove from the tray to cool.

The original chocolate chip cookie recipe has been attributed to Ruth Graves Wakefield.
In the 1930s, she served them at the cosy and popular Toll House Inn.

Calvados-Chocolate Parfait

4–6 servings

INGREDIENTS

5 egg yolks

150 ml water

75 g caster sugar

150 g dark chocolate

2 tbsp cocoa powder

500 ml double cream

4 tbsp calvados

Chocolate figures:

50 g dark chocolate

(2 tbsp calvados to pour on the parfait)

TIP!

The parfait can be prepared the day before serving and keeps for up to a week in the freezer.

1. Beat the egg yolks briefly.

2. Bring the water to the boil and keep boiling until you have a thick syrup, add the calvados moments before the syrup has thickened, but do not let it boil or the alcohol will evaporate. If you add too much alcohol, the parfait will not freeze properly.

3. Immediately beat the calvados syrup into the egg yolks. Keep beating the mixture until it thickens. Then refrigerate.

4. Melt the chocolate in a heat-proof bowl suspended over boiling water or in a microwave oven. Allow to cool, then stir it into the egg mixture together with the cocoa powder.

5. Whip the cream (not too stiff) and fold into the parfait mixture.

6. Pour into serving glasses and freeze for 4 hours.

7. Chocolate garnish: Melt the dark chocolate in a heat-proof bowl suspended over boiling water or in a microwave oven. Fill up a pastry bag with good quality melted chocolate and make meandering lines, latticework, flowers or chains of droplets on a baking parchment and refrigerate until set. Use to garnish your dessert, but remember not to make them too thin and fragile, or they may break.

8. Take the parfait out of the fridge 20 minutes before serving. Garnish with chocolate shapes, berries, chopped nuts or mint leaves, or top with calvados.

Calvados is a kind of apple brandy, an *Appellation d'Origine Contrôlée* from the region of Calvados and a few surrounding regions in Normandy. It is made from a cider distillate, matured in oak casks and enjoyed with coffee, in cocktails, long drinks or on the rocks.

Individual Orange-Chocolate Cakes

Makes 6–8

INGREDIENTS

250 g dark chocolate, 50–70 %

120 g unsalted butter

125 g fine sugar

3 eggs

150 g wheat flour

1 tsp ground cinnamon

1 tsp salt

½ orange

2 tsp vanilla-flavoured icing sugar

Filling:

Candied orange peel or marmalade

Garnish:

Orange

Vanilla-flavoured icing sugar

1. **Preparation:** Preheat the oven to 180 °C (gas mark 4). Butter a few heart-shaped baking tins. Melt the dark chocolate in a heat-proof bowl suspended over boiling water or in a microwave oven.

2. Beat sugar and eggs in a large bowl. Add the softened butter, flour, salt, cinnamon, vanilla-flavoured icing sugar and add a little fresh juice from half an orange. Stir in the melted chocolate.

3. Distribute the mixture into the moulds about half way up, add a piece of candied orange peel (or 1 tbsp marmalade) in each mould. Add the rest of the mixture on top. The moulds should be filled to approximately ¾.

4. Bake for approximately 25 minutes until completely set. Allow to rest in the mould before turning out.

Serve with half an orange slice and sprinkle over a little icing sugar.

The word 'orange' has entered the English language via Old French, and long before that an ancient Indian language. Later, it also came to refer to the colour of the fruit.

Heart Macaroons

Makes 16–20

INGREDIENTS

Macaroons:

120 g ground almonds

200 g icing sugar

1 tsp vanilla-flavoured icing sugar

50 g cocoa powder

100 g egg white (approx. 3 whites)

50 g sugar

Garnish:

25 g white chocolate

25 g dark chocolate

TIP!

The macaroons can be filled with vanilla custard or any other delicious creamy filling.

1. Preheat the oven to 170 °C (gas mark 3). Line a biscuit sheet with baking parchment.

2. Mix the ground almonds, icing sugar, vanilla-flavoured icing sugar and cocoa powder in a separate bowl.

3. Whisk the egg whites until stiff and add the sugar, continue whisking for another minute. Fold in the almond, sugar and cocoa mixture.

4. Pour the mixture into a pastry bag and pipe out the macaroons on the biscuit sheet.

5. Bake for 12–15 minutes. Leave to cool and remove the parchment.

6. Chocolate hearts: Fill a pastry bag with good-quality, melted chocolate and fill some heart-shaped plastic moulds. Add a flavouring of your choice to the chocolate if desired. Leave to set in the fridge and use to decorate the cookies.

Cocoa beans taste differently depending on where they were cultivated and the type of insect that pollinated the flowers. Some cocoa beans taste naturally of vanilla, or even butterscotch. Cocoa beans from Ecuador have a 'flowery' aroma suitable for elegant desserts and pralines.

Stracciatella Mousse

4–6 servings

INGREDIENTS

250 g quark cheese

60 g icing sugar

100 g dark chocolate

200 ml double cream

1 tsp vanilla-flavoured icing sugar

TIP!

Divide the mixture between 3 bowls (without adding the chocolate). Put dark chocolate in one, mashed raspberries in the second and milk chocolate and a few drops of rum in the third. Serve in small bowls or shots glasses so everyone can get a taste.

1. Mix together quark cheese, icing sugar and 50 g of the chopped chocolate.

2. Whip the cream and fold into the mixture.

3. Pour into dessert bowls or glasses and refrigerate for 30 minutes.

4. Chocolate shavings: Use a potato peeler to shave decorative spirals from the edges of a chocolate bar that has been left out at room temperature.

Back in the 17th century, Madame de Sévigné once mentioned to her daughter that chocolate could have strange side effects. 'The Marquise de C drank too much chocolate when she was with child last year so she gave birth to a little boy that was as black as the devil.'

Mint Chocolate Cake

12 mini cakes

INGREDIENTS

Base:

3 eggs

300 g sugar

150 g butter

75 g cocoa powder

125 g wheat flour

1 tsp vanilla-flavoured icing sugar

1 tsp baking powder

Chocolate cream:

250 ml cream

200 g best dark chocolate 70 %

100 g mint chocolate (e.g. After Eight, 12 squares)

30 g unsalted butter

Garnish:

Fresh strawberries

Lemon balm

Vanilla-flavoured icing sugar

Grated chocolate

TIP!

The cake will turn out even better if you bake it the day before so that the chocolate, mint and cocoa flavours have time to develop. Serve with something tangy to balance the chocolate, for example raspberries, mango, passion fruit, or why not a couple of spoonfuls of citrus fruit salad.

1. Preheat the oven to 180 °C (gas mark 4).

2. Whisk the egg and sugar for at least 3 minutes. Melt the butter over a low flame. Remove from the heat and whisk in the cocoa powder.

3. Fold the cocoa butter into the egg mixture and add wheat flour, baking powder and vanilla-flavoured sugar.

4. Butter and flour the sides and bottom of a square loose-bottomed tin, 15 x 15 cm or larger, and pour in the mixture. Bake for about 35 minutes.

Chocolate cream:

5. Slowly melt butter, cream, dark chocolate and mint chocolate in a saucepan. Remove the saucepan from the heat and cool at room temperature. The mixture should be thick and creamy.

6. Allow the cake to cool completely before cutting it into 12 pieces. Cover the tops and sides in chocolate cream.

Serve with strawberries, lemon balm, a little vanilla-flavoured icing sugar and grated chocolate.

This is the perfect cake for all fans of chocolate – and you do not even have to share it with anyone else! Each piece is individually covered in chocolate cream. Long live egotism!

Petits Choux

Makes 12

INGREDIENTS

50 g unsalted butter

150 ml water

60 g wheat flour

2 eggs

A pinch of salt

Filling:

300 ml double cream

1–2 tbsp vanilla-flavoured icing sugar

Decoration:

100 g dark chocolate, 50 %

20 g butter

1 tbsp golden syrup

2 tbsp water

Petits choux dough:

1. **Preparation:** Preheat the oven to 200 °C (gas mark 6). Cover a large biscuit sheet in baking parchment. Melt the butter together with the salt and water. Bring to the boil and remove from the heat.

2. Whisk in the flour and continue to whisk vigorously until the dough no longer adheres to the sides of the bowl. Allow to cool slightly. Fold in the eggs, one at a time until you have a shiny, smooth mixture.

3. Pipe out 7 cm strings onto the tray. Leave some space in between for them to expand. Bake until they are golden brown and risen, approx. 25 minutes. Do not open the oven door during the first 10 minutes to prevent the dough from deflating.

4. Make a slit along the side of each string and return to the oven for 3 minutes. Transfer to a wire cooling rack and leave to cool

Filling:

5. Whip the cream and vanilla-flavoured icing sugar until fluffy. Pipe the mixture into the petits choux.

Decorate:

6. Heat chocolate, butter, syrup and water gently over low heat in a thick-bottomed saucepan. Make decorative swirls with the help of a brush on top of the petits choux.

Petit chou is French for 'small cabbage'. If you have more than one, *petits choux* is the correct spelling.

Chocolate Fudge Fondue

4–6 servings

INGREDIENTS

For the dip:

150 g Muscovado sugar

50 g unsalted butter

200 g dark chocolate, chopped, 70 %

1 tsp vanilla-flavoured icing sugar

100 ml sour cream

Fruits for dipping:

Pineapple

Pear

Mango

Physalis

Seedless green grapes

Strawberries

E.g. cookies, marshmallows or even hard cheese

Wooden skewers or cocktail sticks

1. Gently heat the sugar together with 100 ml water until the sugar has dissolved. Bring to the boil and boil for four minutes until dark and syrupy.

2. Remove the saucepan from the heat and immediately submerge it in cold water. Add 2 tbsp water – Warning: use a splashguard or stand well back.

3. Return the saucepan to the stove and simmer while stirring until the syrup has turned smooth and shiny.

4. Stir in the butter, chocolate and vanilla-flavoured icing sugar and stir until melted. Stir in the sour cream. Set aside.

5. Peel and cut bite-size pieces of pineapple, pears, mango and cheese. Pull the physalis husks over the top of the berry and wring tight to form a handle.

6. Reheat the sauce. It should be warm but not too hot. Serve in one large bowl or several individual bowls.

There are many rules that need to be observed when eating fondue in Switzerland. If a man should drop a piece of bread into the oil, he must treat the party to a bottle of wine. If a woman should do the same, she must kiss the man on her left.

A Grand Chocolate Cake

12 slices

INGREDIENTS

Base:
200 g almonds, skins removed
300 g of the best dark chocolate
2 tsp cocoa powder
6 eggs
200 g unsalted butter, at room temperature
100 g sugar
A pinch of salt

Vanilla custard:
1 vanilla pod
200 ml double cream
60 g icing sugar
4 egg yolks
200 ml quark cheese

White chocolate sauce:
200 ml cream
200 g white chocolate, chopped

Icing:
150 g dark chocolate, crushed

Serving and garnishing:
150 g fresh raspberries
Dark chocolate shavings
Lemon balm

1. Preheat the oven to 190 ºC (gas mark 5).

2. Line the bottom of a loose-bottomed tin (approx. 20 cm) with a baking parchment, butter the sides and sprinkle with flour or cocoa powder.

Vanilla custard:
3. Slit the vanilla pod down the middle, scrape the seeds into a saucepan and add the rest of the pod. Bring the cream and sugar to the boil and remove immediately from the heat. Take out the vanilla pod and whisk in the egg yolks. Simmer on low heat until the cream thickens. Allow to cool, whisk in the quark cheese. Refrigerate for 1 hour.

Base:
4. Grind the almonds finely in a food processor. Add chocolate and cocoa powder, and process for 1 minute. Transfer the almond-chocolate mixture to a large bowl.

5. Separate the eggs.

6. Whisk together butter, sugar and salt until fluffy, then add the egg yolks, one at a time. Pour over the almond mixture and mix well.

7. Take out a clean bowl and whisk the egg whites until stiff. Fold into the chocolate mixture. Pour into the buttered tin and bake in the lower half of the oven for 50 minutes. It should be dry in the middle. Leave to cool completely before removing the tin. Use a sharp knife and cut the cake into three round slices.

8. Mash the raspberries into a pulp, but leave a few that can be used for decoration.

9. Put one base on a plate and spread first with raspberry purée and then with a layer of vanilla custard. Put another base on top and continue adding raspberry purée and custard. Place the third base on top.

Icing:
10. Melt the chocolate in a heat-proof bowl suspended over boiling water or in a microwave oven. Spread or pipe the melted dark chocolate over the whole cake. Refrigerate for an hour so the flavours can develop.

Chocolate sauce:
11. Heat the cream. Place the chopped white chocolate in a bowl and pour over the warm cream. Stir until you have a thick sauce.

Serve the cake topped with dark chocolate shavings, fresh raspberries and lemon balm.

Peanut Cookies

Makes 30–40

INGREDIENTS

Cookie dough:

200 g butter

175 g sugar

2 tbsp golden syrup

1 tsp baking powder

250 g wheat flour

200 g shelled, finely crushed peanuts

Candied nuts:

150 g shelled peanuts

50 g sugar

20 g unsalted butter

Chocolate icing:

150 g good-quality dark chocolate

TIP!

We have used peanuts, but you can use any type of nut: hazelnuts, almonds, walnuts, pecans or Brazil nuts – pick your favourite!

1. Preheat the oven to 180 °C (gas mark 4). Line a biscuit sheet with a baking parchment.

2. Mix the butter, syrup and sugar, mix in the finely crushed peanuts, flour and baking powder.

3. Form into a sausage and slice. Place the slices well apart on the baking tray.

4. Bake for 11–13 minutes. Allow to cool on the biscuit sheet for a few minutes before sprinkling over the candied nuts and pipe over the chocolate icing.

Candied nuts:

5. Shell the nuts and roast them in a dry frying pan until golden.

6. Melt the butter, add the sugar and heat slowly until golden. Make sure the sugar does not burn! Add the roasted, peeled peanuts and stir so that every nut is covered in sugar. Make sure they do not burn! If you like, you can add some cinnamon or cardamom to the sugar mixture.

7. Sprinkle the nuts over the cookies before they have cooled and become hard.

Chocolate icing:

8. Melt the chocolate in a heat-proof bowl suspended over boiling water or microwave oven. Pipe decorative swirls over the nuts. Allow to cool before serving.

A peanut is in fact not a nut; it is the extremely nutritious seed of the peanut plant. Peanuts only contain 50 % fat, most of it unsaturated. Peanuts go very well with chocolate. In 2008, as much as 20 % of the harvest worldwide was claimed by chocolate manufacturers.

Spicy Chocolate Muffins

Makes 12

INGREDIENTS

150 g milk chocolate

250 g wheat flour

175 g brown sugar

2 tsp baking powder

2 tsp ground cinnamon

1 tsp ground ginger

1 tsp ground cloves

1 tsp ground black pepper

1 tsp ground cardamom

1 tsp finely shredded orange zest

2 eggs

200 ml sour cream

100 g unsalted butter + 20 g for the tin, at room temperature

1. Preheat the oven to 190 ºC (gas mark 5). Thoroughly butter a non-stick muffin tin, and do not forget the rim since the muffins will rise up over the edge. Do not use baking parchment or paper cups.

2. Mix wheat flour, baking powder, cinnamon, ginger, cloves, pepper, cardamom and orange zest in a bowl.

3. Melt the chocolate in a heat-proof bowl suspended over boiling water or in a microwave oven. Leave to cool a little.

4. Mix until smooth and shiny.

5. Fill up the muffin tins nearly all the way up. Bake at the centre of the oven for 20 minutes.

These muffins are intense. Use less spices and omit the black pepper for a milder version.

The word 'muffin' is believed to derive from the German 'muffe', which means 'cake'.
This is a slightly different version, which is smaller than the American version.

Classic Chocolate Sauce

INGREDIENTS

300 ml milk

2 tbsp bitter cocoa powder

85 g sugar

2 egg yolks

1. Whisk the egg yolks and sugar until fluffy. Add the milk and cocoa powder, continue whisking.

2. Pour everything into a saucepan. Bring to the boil and remove from the heat.

Serve cold – it is best straight out of the fridge.

Creamy Chocolate Sauce

INGREDIENTS

50 g cocoa powder

175 g sugar

300 ml cream

1 tsp vanilla-flavoured icing sugar

1. Put everything in a saucepan and bring almost to the boil. Lower the heat.

2. Simmer for 6–10 minutes. Ready!

Can be served hot or cold.

Dark Chocolate Sauce

INGREDIENTS

300 ml single cream

1 tbsp cornstarch

300 g good, dark grated chocolate, min. 50 %

1. Whisk together the cold cream and cornstarch over medium heat.

2. Remove the saucepan and add the chocolate. Stir until the chocolate has melted.

Serve immediately – it tastes best warm.

Cocoa beans were the main currency in Central America in the 16th and 17th centuries. Gold and silver were used too, but contrary to cocoa beans, they could not be used everywhere.

Milk Chocolate Sauce

INGREDIENTS

200 ml milk

2 tsp vanilla-flavoured icing sugar

60 g milk chocolate, grated

30 g dark chocolate, grated

2 tbsp icing sugar

2 egg yolks

1 tsp cornstarch

1. Heat up the milk in a saucepan. Remove from the stove and add the chocolate. Give it a stir now and then until the chocolate has melted. Set aside.

2. Whisk egg yolks and icing sugar in a separate bowl and add the cornstarch.

3. Pour the egg mixture into the chocolate mixture and simmer a few minutes while stirring. Set aside to cool.

White Chocolate Sauce

INGREDIENTS

1 vanilla pod

200 ml cream

2 tbsp icing sugar

150 g white chocolate, chopped

1. Slit the vanilla pod down the middle and scrape the seeds into a saucepan. Add the rest of the pod too. Simmer the cream and icing sugar for a few minutes. Remove the creamy mixture from the heat and cool slightly. Remove the vanilla pod.

2. Put the chocolate in a separate bowl and pour on the warm vanilla cream. Stir until smooth.

Serve while it is still warm.

Most people think of fine chocolate as dark chocolate, which is correct: Fine chocolate is always dark. However, many self-proclaimed experts tend to go for as high cocoa content as possible, which is not the best thing to do since the chocolate will not taste any better the more solids it contains. 75 % is about right; higher concentrations leave a bitter taste.

From the same publisher

THE COCKTAIL BOOK

Fancy a cocktail party? Now you have the chance to mix all your favourite drinks at home!

Here you will find more than 250 different cocktail recipes. The selection of cocktails is intended as an inspiration for the novice as well as the more experienced home bartender. The cocktails vary in number of ingredients and complexity of preparation, but they have one thing in common – they're delicious!

The Cocktail Book includes a section on glass types and equipment and advices you on which spirits, liqueurs and juices to use. You will also find a thorough guide to all the technical terms and expressions used in bartending, a comprehensive history of alcoholic beverages and a fascinating account of the manufacturing of spirits. Each drink recipe is accompanied by trivia and fun facts, often relating to the historical people and myths surrounding the drinks. There simply can be no cocktail book without Mr Hemingway!

The book is aimed towards the wide population of cocktail lovers. It contains all the old classics, but also plenty of trendy novelties. You will find the old familiar cocktails in many new guises, often with an international, exciting flavour.

In short, this a complete collection of cocktails ideal for surprising your friends on a Saturday night, but also for boosting your own cocktail skills and knowledge!

ISBN 978-1-908233-05-9

From the same publisher

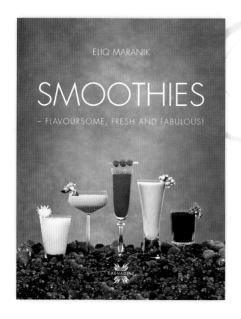

SMOOTHIES
– flavoursome, fresh and fabulous!

Here comes the ultimate compendium for anyone waiting to be inspired to have fun in the kitchen with fruit and veg and create tasty, nutritious fruit drinks. *Smoothies* contains more than 100 recipes of all kinds, such as frozen summer smoothies, health-boosting juices and shots, or how about some lovely homemade fruit yoghurt? Fancy something less wholesome? There are plenty of sinfully delicious milkshakes and desserts just waiting to be tested. Add some liqueur, and your smoothie turns into a seductive cocktail.

Smoothies maintains a clear organic perspective throughout and aims to inspire the reader to think organically, locally and seasonally when buying fruit. The book offers you a complete guide to the fruit section in shops and supermarkets, and anyone who has ever asked themselves why we really bother eating fruit and veg will find a complete guide to fruit as a bountiful source of vitamins, minerals and antioxidants. The book is full of advice on how to succeed with home blending as well as useful information of what to think about when choosing equipment. In short, a real bible for the fruit and veg lover – everything you need to know!

ISBN 978-1-908233-06-6

WHISKY & FOOD

Jan Groth is Global Scotch Brand Ambassador for the largest group of whisky producers in the world. He feels privileged to be able to teach people everything they need to know about whisky, learn from the best in the business and discuss food and whisky with chefs and celebrities.

In this book, Jan Groth describes his own and other people's favourite whiskies. It is a cookery book in disguise, in which foods and flavours are communicated through anecdotes and travel accounts in a most delicious way. It also includes useful tips on how whisky and food work together as well as a multitude of mouth watering whisky-inspired recipes by professional chefs.

This book is full of great pictures by Arne Adler of equally great food photographed in scenic inland and seaside locations across Scotland. Inspiring recipes and top of the line whiskies such as Talisker, Caol Ila and Ardbeg contribute to the pleasures of combining food and whisky, turning us all into whisky ambassadors. Slainté Maith! Dinner is served.

ISBN 978-1-908233-04-2

hothomes
Suzanne Trocmé

hothomes

Suzanne Trocmé

Photography by Andrew Wood

jacqui
small

First published in 2006 by
Jacqui Small LLP,
an imprint of Aurum Books,
25 Bedford Avenue, London
WC1B 3AT

Text copyright © Suzanne
Trocmé 2006
Design and layout copyright ©
Jaqui Small 2006

Publisher: Jacqui Small
Editorial Manager: Kate John
Designer: Lawrence Morton
Editor: Catherine Rubinstein
Production: Peter Colley

ISBN-10: 1 903221 40 4
ISBN-13: 978 1 903221 40 2

A catalogue record for this book
is available from the British
Library.

2008 2007 2006
10 9 8 7 6 5 4 3 2 1

Printed in Singapore

contents

controlling
the environment

Global warming is coming to us all, despite ongoing debate as to the details of its impact. Add to that the fact that increasing numbers of temperate-dwellers are adopting warm-climate second homes as an escape from modern life, and it becomes essential to adapt to hot living, to do so sustainably and with style.

In a hot land, the aim is both to minimise the impact of the heat and to take advantage of its benefits: to even out its extremes and take shelter from the worst of it, at the same time as using its energy to best effect in terms of power consumption. Throughout the whole process of creating a home, from initial choice of terrain, through selection of specific site and orientation, to choice of materials and even details such as colour, heat is a prime consideration. The challenge can be met through lo-tech and largely passive means – age-old methods of building or ventilating – as much as through modern and interventionist techniques; and along with stemming rising temperatures, it is important not to overlook the value of creating an ambience of cool calm even when the actuality is otherwise.

There is no such thing, however, as an ultimate sustainable or environmentally friendly building system. Each project, each site, each building must be approached on an individual basis: in other words, a holistic approach that looks at all the factors that impact on a site, the occupants, its region, climate, culture and resources, before a strategy is employed. The site will have its own microclimate, affected by surrounding terrain, buildings, elevation, vegetation and so on. Knowing all these factors can help a designer orientate a building to take advantage of them, turning it to catch the sun or wind, or shifting it a few degrees so that tall trees provide shade. According to a build's surroundings and the owner's priorities, choices will be made, for instance to avoid or gain sun.

Aspect not only concerns views, therefore, but an entire quagmire of devices required to set up orientation of a home so it functions successfully both against and with the elements. The aim is to control the environment.

Orientation is the first consideration, since it determines where you build your home and in which direction it faces. Designer Andrzej Zarzycki spent five days with his clients driving around their South African game farm near the Botswana border before deciding where exactly the house should be built (see pages 30–3). They chose the perfect spot: the principal house, a labyrinth of lodges, stands on a hillside overlooking the most exquisite plain for game watching – and directly at the favourite watering hole of local baboon; they also have a penchant for game watching, so now the swimming pool has become the first port of call for the baboon, who frequently join the owners for breakfast! Not so much a mistake as a wise and instinctive decision which possibly indicates that we are closer to nature than we might imagine when it comes to house-building!

The most obvious way to keep a home cool is to prevent it heating up too much in the first place. In any terrain, simple design strategies can be employed to minimise heat gain from the sun by having sufficient shelter from it. Siting a structure in the shade of a hillside or trees, sinking it deep into the ground, or building it with thick walls and insulating materials (such as local stone) can all be effective techniques for keeping cool, and basic siting can be amended with details such as overhanging eaves or foliage. As Frank Lloyd Wright put it, "The physician can bury his mistakes, but the architect can only advise his client to plant vines."

Size and positioning of windows is also fundamental. Very few of the houses covered in this book have windows of similar size all the way round the perimeter walls. While in temperate climes we may crave sun, in hot homes we are mostly trying to keep it out, or at least control it. Sometimes large picture windows are used only on the side of the house where there is the least direct sun – preferably along with the best view, or the waterside if there is water – with tiny windows, mere slits, in the sunniest wall, in order to keep out the fierce summer light and heat. In the environs of dusty Marrakech, however, we found the home of architect Karim El Achak (see pages 54–9) positioned to have large southerly windows so that the sun is present in the wintertime, and for the view of the Atlas Mountains. South-facing in California or the Mediterranean, for instance, may be too hot, but where the summer sun is directly overhead, nearer the equator, as El Achak points out, it does not enter the house at all. In such cases it may actually be late-afternoon sun from the west that provides the most solar heat gain. The point is there is no single correct approach; it is important to weigh up all factors and choose your priorities.

Sunlight is of course our friend as well as our enemy – we just have to know when to say "no" and shut it out or live in penumbra. In some cases we may choose to use solar power to drive heating and even cooling systems, either by passive means such as solar windows (see page 135) or by more active methods, most typically solar panels (although these can be expensive), and this too will affect siting of windows.

Windows are also fundamental to ventilation, especially essential in humid heat. Air conditioning is not the obvious answer it may seem, since it generates greenhouse gases; systems with the highest emissions are beginning to be restricted by building regulations in the EU and USA, and are likely to be further constrained in the future. Our natural cooling systems are water and air, and there are many ways to use them. Aside from positioning openings so that they encourage through draughts, some deceptively simple cooling systems have evolved over time, and there is much to be learned from indigenous or vernacular architecture, a valuable basis for "green" design, within the tropics and in other parts of the world.

The traditional Malay house and the Ibans' longhouses of Southeast Asia are good examples. Both are wooden structures set on posts, with steep roofs and high ceilings, designs that mean good ventilation and cooling of interior spaces. Being up on stilts allows ventilation beneath the buildings, keeps living spaces above the flood line and limits the possibility of invasion

aspect is key to siting a hot home; a minor adjustment to orientation can make a huge difference. **RIGHT, TOP** The concrete back of the property in Plettenberg Bay in South Africa (see pages 70–3): note the lack of windows on this north-facing, i.e. sunny, side. The house is orientated towards the beach and the upper section is pivoted over the lower to take maximum advantage of the view. **RIGHT, BOTTOM** To build on a hill looking out to sea may mean waiting for the right piece of real estate to become available. There is no second-best. The Na Xemena house in Ibiza (see pages 86–91) has an unprecedented view, and the hills and water allow natural cooling of the interior and exterior spaces. There is in fact a property just beneath, which is not overlooked due to clever orientation.

by predators. The materials tend to be lightweight and therefore do not retain heat. Recently these traditional designs have been reinterpreted in more contemporary designs that utilise passive energy strategies.

In the Middle East, the ancient cooling towers known as *badgir* in Persian are still to be found in Iran, and are still cool inside when it is 38°C (100°F) outside. The simplest towers are rectangular, containing shafts with two to four shelves: the upper shelves catch incoming hot air and redirect it out again, while the lower ones recirculate cool air from inside. Air is cooled further by passing over a pool of water. The region's traditional skills with engineering are also evident in irrigation systems based on natural underground water channels; found from Morocco to Central Asia, they are called *karez* in the Xinjiang region of western China and *qanats* in Persia, where they originated. With skills like these, it is not surprising that by the 13th century the Islamic garden, for all its arid location, from the Alhambra in Spain to the Taj Mahal in India, was such a stunning success. Water featured heavily, as did canopies of fruit trees that restricted re-radiation losses from the ground, trapping cool air that could be circulated through the house – another form of natural cooling.

Water can be a friend to cool any home by way of a pool, a water feature, or a vista of sea or lake. Although I am a firm believer that a pool is useless if you live in the UK, it is an absolute necessity in a warm climate, should water not be entirely scarce. Not only does it refresh all through the day – a quick dip is all it takes – but the mere presence of water is a tonic. A lake can bring a breeze, gentle or otherwise, and the ocean brings zest of life (and negative ions to boot) and the most delightful sounds too. Water heats up much more slowly than air, so it remains cooler when the surrounding air is hot. It enables vegetation to grow, which in turn gives us shade and, together with the water, increases rates of evaporation. This is part of the reason that rural areas are cooler than urban ones: heat is lost in evaporation from streams and rivers and transpiration from trees (another reason is that concrete retains heat). Water can also be used to store heat.

light draws people, as it does flowers, but our need for light must be balanced with keeping cool. **LEFT, 1** In Marrakech small windows help keep the light out. **2** In dark shade in Johannesburg, a dining table comes to life with light streaming from deep ceiling recesses. **3** In Ibiza, a shaft of light is directed by a ceiling skylight in a double-height room; although bright, it is gentle. **4** Old and new architecture can coexist without apology, light bringing both to life. In Provence the light dances through a basket arbour. **5** "There are frequently links between the ecology of a building ... and the poetic dimensions of architecture – such as the fleeting effect of shadow patterns.... Perhaps one should define them under the heading of 'lifting the spirits'", says Sir Norman Foster. Seth Stein in South Africa creates extraordinary pattern, with echoes of arbours. **6** Tall slit windows throw light onto an interior wall in North Africa for reflected light; the room remains cool. **7** White reflects light and helps spread it evenly. **8** Light, air and sunshine were the new ideals in the Neues Bauen movement of the 1920s. Thirty years later, glass buildings became a reality, with air conditioning to regulate internal climate. **9** The rear of this house, a series of *fincas*, has small windows; its opposite side has window walls facing out to sea. **RIGHT** Nature, when manipulated, can find the best solutions to harsh sunlight, and vines and creepers will meld a home into its environment.

Building or adapting a home in a humid environment differs vastly from building in an arid one. Water can become the enemy when rot sets in if incorrect materials have been used. Local and indigenous ones are always best, built by nature to cope – look for hardwoods such as teak (a tip for updating a bathroom in any climate) and porous stone (so as not to slip).

A seminal building that truly represents well-thought-out orientation, not just for the choice of waterside position but also its structure, which takes advantage of such a position, thus the vision of the building itself, is the Sydney Opera House. Following a competition in 1956, the project was built by the Danish Jorn Utzon between 1957 and 1973. Utzon said in 2004, "In the construction process, we study the sources of human wellbeing more than anyone else.... The partner is thus in the broad sense *the place*. On land it's about a site and some surroundings – it may be a forest or a plain, with the wind conditions and the light that the place happens to offer, but at all events it's a partner that you have to relate to."

Two other successful waterside buildings that appeal to me enormously are Frank Gehry's titanium-tiled Guggenheim Museum in Bilbao, built in the city's docklands, and the earlier Malaparte house built by Groupe 7 on the Italian island of Capri. Like the Opera House, Bilbao is a gateway building, and Gehry struggled with its scale. It is a museum, I know, and huge, and self-confessedly metaphorical, but it feels completely human – a successful, "living" waterside development which, despite its dizzying undulating form, enhances the environment as well as protecting from it.

Casa Malaparte, built for writer Curzio Malaparte in the late 1930s, is a very friendly house on a steep cliff over water and was the first to incorporate the picture window – a picture-frame window where the view becomes the art. It does not follow any of the island's building manners, does nothing to camouflage itself, but nevertheless you cannot imagine any other place where it could have been built. Strong and marked lines, bulks added one upon another in a modular way, emphasise the rationalist origin of the architectural concept the building is based upon. A blueprint for modern waterside living, Malaparte used to be open to the public but now has a tenant – so as much as I urge you to visit both Bilbao and Sydney, I am afraid Malaparte will have to elude you, apart from in books.

These three examples all make use of platforms or levels. Aspect involves volume and cannot be thought of in a rectilinear manner. Platforms are used to pull people through buildings, whether public or private, and create fluidity. As air has to circulate, so do people to make the best of a hot home. In Ibiza and North Africa we came across houses built as *enfilades* of boxes, either linked by a common hallway or built in the manner of Versailles, one box flowing from another over changing levels. In the south of France the house height had to be contained by local building restrictions, so the plan shows a leisurely incline upwards using subtle platforms. In other schemes, spaces were hollowed out to provide escape from the elements. Spatial continuity minimises the sense of enclosure.

air & water are our natural cooling systems. **BELOW** Water takes longer to change temperature, either upward or downward, than land does, so water is cooler than land by day and warmer by night. Air temperature is influenced by the land or water beneath it, and this difference in temperature, and consequently pressure, results in breezes: from water to land by day and from land to water by night. This is Merimbula on Australia's Sapphire Coast: architect Clinton Murray likes louvres, which assist air flow. **OPPOSITE** Vertical air circulation occurs when air heats up. Its molecules spread out and it becomes less dense than surrounding unheated air; it therefore rises, transferring its heat to a cooler region and allowing cool air to take its place – this is heat transfer by convection. Fans, seen here in a double-height room (good for convection) in Provence by Andrzej Zarzycki, also encourage air flow.

For nomadic populations space is rarely a problem, but water is imperative. The Rendille, for example, are African nomadic pastoralists whose movements are dictated by the need for forage and water for their camels – they live in the desert between the Ndoto mountains of Kenya and Lake Turkana. On finding water, Rendille women construct their home, a *min*, which has been carried in kit form by camel. This bent-pole and stick framework with sisal panels forms a kind of whelk shape: two-thirds of a hemisphere with an inclined front, not unlike the some of our super-sized family tents. At the rear, a couple of animal hides are hung for shade, although they can be removed if the interior becomes too stifling. On plan, the *min* departs from the circle, being wider at the front than the rear. It is a delightful architectural shape. Although it quivers (it is lightweight, for transportation) in the fierce winds that come off Lake Turkana, this waterside structure is nevertheless sturdy and successful as shelter against heat and dust as well as wind. So sensitive are the Rendille to the environment, they take care not to overgraze land or pollute water. We should take heed on many counts. The structure not only behaves well in the elements, but is positioned directionally and aerodynamic in form. Despite ranting daylight temperatures in such regions, it is the lake that provides the most problematic condition: the wind. It seems ironic that the Rendille spend their lives seeking water, yet water becomes their enemy.

I believe that building cannot be looked at in isolation, and the core of this book explores living in a hot climate by terrain. Whether we aspire to hot-house living or have it coming to us through global warming, it is better to be prepared and see how the professionals do it, to look to the world.

terrain

LEFT A double-height structure – or a tall building – of earth or adobe is structurally impossible but can be delightful in a hot climate for air movement. In order to build a tall property, KO architects used structural concrete beams as support for the earth walls.

THIS PAGE Rugs are mainly Moroccan from the Atlas Mountains or Berber – wool has a capacity for keeping cool in the summer and warm in the winter. Soft seating is made from pigskin.

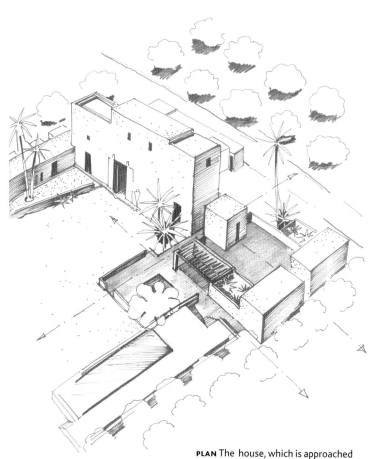

PLAN The house, which is approached from the rear, faces the Atlas Mountains. The structure is the only building visible – barren land lies beyond it. Olives and palms, on the whole imported, line the perimeter of the site.

the main door leads past the children's quarter, the house unfolding later on – a demure arrival into a rather large property, unlike a huge front door and bells chiming magnificence. I would rather experience unfolding pleasures.

At the opposite end of the building, a group of small detached cubes form guest suites, masterful in contemporary simplicity. Outdoor relaxation areas, one a pergola with a planted bamboozerie and one on the roof, are shaded by dried palm leaves and white cotton drapes.

From outside, the walls are almost the colour of the ground, not the pinker tone more usually seen locally: soil was brought in from another region to alter the colour so the house appears as a mirage. (There is nothing around at all – our directions were to turn off the road at a Coca Cola sign and look for a building.) This is a modern house made of ancient materials. The walls, so thick that heat cannot possibly permeate, are raw-earth brick (comprising earth, straw and various minerals), pressed and then sun-dried. The exterior is coated in rough earth and straw, interior walls in polished earth and straw, stablised with oil. Ceilings are a plaster-earth mix.

Floors are concrete, varnished with anthracite-coloured concrete, which is also on walls and ceilings in the bathrooms. Concrete is used too for structural beams, permitting creation of large rooms – double height for air circulation – which would have been almost impossible with only earth.

Because of the intense, overhead sunlight, the windows are narrow, elongated slits, allowing in just shafts of light and little heat; the only large opening is to the south, with a view to the mountains. Rooms remain in penumbra, their darkness enhanced by the dark tones of the walls.

Doors and furniture make use of iroko wood, chestnut and iron, all simply waxed. Fireplaces and Berber rugs in natural, undyed wools (the black diamond pattern is from black sheep) provide warmth. Curiously, on those rare occasions when the fire is lit, the mountains are reflected in the glass of one of the fireplaces, the snow "melting" in the fire. Fournier admits this was an accident, but very little else appears accidental. Primitive this is not: for two young architects it is a magnificent *oeuvre*.

ABOVE The pool is a welcome respite at any time of day in the desert. The air is exceedingly dry and it is very easy to dehydrate. Any water feels refreshing. Here you feel as if you are away from civilisation for good.

ABOVE CENTRE The four children's quarters, in strict uniformity (each child has a small integral terrace). Exterior walls are made from sun-dried raw-earth bricks, finished with a coating of straw and rough earth..

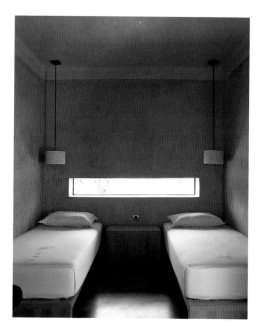

ABOVE RIGHT Inside a child's bedroom. Each child has two beds in case they have a guest. As well as a row of washbasins, there is a shower room in the children's wing. Inside is for sleeping and outdoors for playing.

RIGHT Roof terraces remain the coolest spot for evening dining although this ground-level relaxation and dining area gives some respite from daytime sun. The Atlas Mountains are just beyond but cannot be seen in high-summer haze.

(CASE STUDY)

Fair game "It is not easy installing a new Africa into Africa," says designer Andrzej Zarzycki, "but the mere commissioning of local pieces and materials from local weavers means that we have an authentic, although quite sophisticated, interior." The exterior, a game farm in the South African bush, takes care of itself.

When lengthy driving directions include the words, "Drive on for about 100 km [60 miles], you will eventually see a green sign: slow down, you are almost there," you know you are in the wild. Once on the property, the vast scale is still apparent, with a good ten-minute drive to the house, visible from the road at times, high up on the hill. Along the road, zebra, kudu and giraffe pop in and out of sight.

The private game farm (where big game are raised for viewing) in the Northern Province on the road to Thabazimbi that London-based interior designer Andrzej Zarzycki has had the pleasure of creating with his clients contains a host of buildings: dwellings for support staff – gamekeepers, trackers, house staff – as well as a second (or third or fourth) home for the well-travelled and exuberant clients. There are two principal Zarzycki-designed buildings: the main house, built in collaboration with architect

Colin Milliken, which takes the form of a grouping of guest cottages (simple sleep cells feature greatly in hot houses, since most of the living is outdoors; here each bedroom has its own sitting room and bathroom), winging one way and then the other from a central core where entertaining takes place; and, along a dirt track, another very smart but smaller house which offers respite for the host from energetic guests and omnipresent animal life – although it too has its share of visitors, as vervet monkeys dramatically appear at the small house's pool each morning and giraffe stroll close by.

Zarzycki is partner to Anthony Collett in the practice Collett-Zarzycki, a 15-year-old architecture and design firm with a 25-strong team as well as a network of outside specialists, artists and craftspeople. Both partners seek to embrace local tradition wherever they can. Zarzycki grew up in Zambia and knows the sights and sounds of Africa well although, having trained and practised mainly in Europe, this is his first game-farm project.

The property was originally a 2,000ha (5,000-acre) cattle farm, half on flat land and half in the hills. The owner, on finding his own slice of South Africa, decided to stock it with non-predatory animals so he and his wife and family could safely walk around without the threat of wild cats.

This house is not designed to impress and makes no fanfare; the experience is the property as a whole – the view across the plain beneath and the game watching. "If you remove the house from the terrain it is not

OPPOSITE Looking into the main sitting room from the deck. Entry to the house is to the right beyond the African mahogany cabinets. The property is high on a hill and fires are needed on cooler evenings: there is a stone hearth in the centre of the far wall.

ABOVE Looking from the main sitting room out to the deck, and beyond it the dining room and, to the right, a breakfast and "sundowner" terrace. Furniture in local woods is designed by Collett-Zarzycki, and raffia, here as lampshades (left), is used throughout. Raffia curtains segregating indoors from outdoors are handmade by local craftswomen.

FAR LEFT Some guest suites have outdoor fireplaces. Thatch is used for roofing as it provides good insulation, keeping out summer heat and trapping it in for winter.

LEFT A series of three descending swimming pools is designed to look as un-manmade as possible, visually linking the different elements of the outside terraces. Baboons tend to join visitors for breakfast, as if it is their own pool!

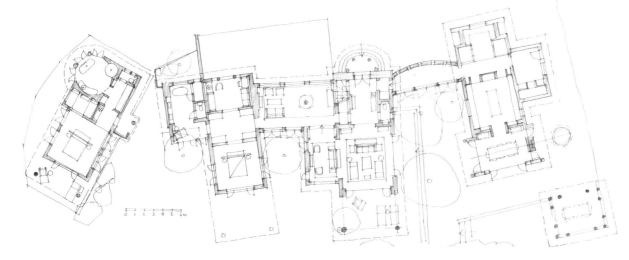

a vast house," comments Zarzycki, "although it does not make sense to remove it since the house is all about the terrain and the mutual acceptance one of the other."

The entrance to the house leads directly into the back of the large south-facing sitting room, with seating arranged to maximise the views through the window wall, which opens entirely onto the deck. The design of the house evolved from its location: it looks outwards and is full of wide openings embracing the view. The uninterrupted transition from inside to out succeeds partly because of the choice of upholstered furniture on the deck, which remains year round: the interior and exterior furnishings follow a similar idiom so distinctions between the two are blurred.

Village-like from the exterior, the units of the house are linked by garden poolside walkways. The series of interlocking rooms flanking the main building are thatched, keeping out summer heat that reaches 40°C (104°F), and trapping warmth in winter, when temperatures drop to freezing

(0°C/32°F). To the north of the house there is a winter room that remains warmer in winter and much lighter than the south-facing side.

Floors throughout the main house are tinted, waxed concrete, while the bedroom cell bathrooms incorporate local granite. Walls are painted in a pale cream distemper, a good background for the contrasting African dark timbers. "The eye is to be drawn outside so we avoided bright colours in favour of neutrals," says the designer. The client was keen to embrace local materials but wanted a quality not usually found outside Johannesburg, and it was a challenge working quite closely with local craftspeople to ensure standards were right, particularly that proportions were adhered to.

Another major challenge was to bring in the amenities, the services, since this was virgin territory. An entirely new drainage system has been set up, with water drawn from boreholes: during periods of drought water is scarce.

Altogether it is a clever house, which at first sight might appear formal. Its informality, however, comes with how it works, its fluidity.

RIGHT Dados in the bathrooms have woven-raffia panels and basins are built into natural rock. Here the bath is an antique pedestal version; those in other suites are more contemporary resin and stone. Each suite has an alfresco shower too.

FAR RIGHT All bedrooms open onto separate balconies with long views. Furniture, including contemporary four-poster beds, is by Collet-Zarzycki in stained mahogany. Mohair bedcovers are by Handworks.

OPPOSITE In the double-height winter room is a Zarzycki-designed table of gum-tree poles bound with rope, with a leather-covered top. Campaign chairs in tan leather are a smart addition to this modern Africanate room. Ceiling fans are invaluable in the heat.

wooded

Perhaps the best surroundings for hot homes are trees. Wooded terrain provides relatively instant solutions to some of the problems of living in overheated climes, offering shade from the onslaught of an overhead sun, shelter against strong winds, a degree of moisture in the air and perhaps even rainfall, and a pleasingly soothing sylvan backdrop for hot, sleepy living. What better sounds as you drift into siesta than the rustling of leaves and the chatter of birds?

The humidity that often accompanies woodland, however, is a mixed blessing: in a humid climate there is no shortage of water, and few problems persuading a garden to grow or creating a cooling water feature but, while we might expect moisture to cool us down, in fact high humidity levels make heat a great deal more enervating and can create a sense of airlessness, as well as exposing building materials to punishing rates of rot, mould, rust and general decay. These are major challenges, requiring targetted solutions and careful choices. Breezes are also an issue, to the extent that simply maintaining a balance between air-conditioned comfort and natural enjoyment of a rainforest environment can be a delicate balancing act.

Fortunately, while forests are inevitably more humid than sparsely vegetated areas, even in hot climates they need not be steaming jungles. Of the homes featured here, one is situated in the humid but not overly hot rainforest of New Zealand's North Island while the other two are both in the manmade rainforest-like setting of a relatively dry location: Johannesburg, high on the plateau grassland of the South African veld.

However humid it may be, forest does provide another challenge – how not to disturb its natural beauty, or indeed fell at all, despite the temptation of on-the-spot building materials. If the site is truly in the depths of a forest, access to roads and utilities may be almost impossible without cutting a scarring swathe through the trees. Architecture in wooded terrain must also be careful not to fight the trees that surround it. Orientation is not as much of an issue as in other terrains, but postioning vis-à-vis the trees is important, both aesthetically and because roots can be disruptive to foundations. It is usually best to use indigenous materials – although true in all climates, this is particularly so in forests because local materials will cope well with moisture: wood or stone brought in from elsewhere is likely to be too porous. Coming from rainforest environments, tropical hardwoods such as teak are especially suited to hot, humid conditions, while other woods – for instance cedar – smell wonderful when hot, whether damp or dry.

Although builds in forests and woods are problematic, they can be the most beautiful for the play of light through the trees. If you can't build in a forest, you can at least capture something of it by building near a few trees, or planting your own. Under a leafy arbour on a hot morning, temperatures can be ten degrees cooler than in the sun. Even in deserts there is that age-old symbol of oasis, the palm tree. When planting palms, be aware that many species cannot tolerate extreme conditions. My personal favourite, the Queen Palm, does badly in cold winters: only fortunate people who live in Palm Springs and other warm-winter areas can enjoy its beauty year round. Palms are essentially architectural. As they mature, many become tall brown columns topped with a giant powder-puff of green. In the long term, shorter palms are generally better for a hint of shade in a hot garden.

OPPOSITE Clifford Forsyth House is a rigorous structure in a leafy New Zealand suburb. Apart from the two angled concrete-block walls that bring shade and privacy, the house consists of thin, laminated timber posts and great expanses of glass infill, a transparency that invites in the trees and belies the suburban location.

Ultimate wood cabin

Arguably one of the most significant houses created in New Zealand in the 20th century is the home architect Patrick Clifford designed for himself in an Auckland suburb: Clifford Forsyth House, built on interesting topography on a sloping triangular plot that ends at a tidal basin. Showing huge courtesy to its environment and appearing essentially made from wood, it is of human scale and compassionate content. Clifford explains: "The built environment plays a major role in the human impact on natural environment and quality of life…. A sustainable design integrates consideration of resource and energy efficiency, healthy buildings and materials, ecologically and socially sensitive land use, and aesthetic sensitivity."

If there is a New Zealand vernacular, this house is its contemporary epitome. But is there one? In the first years of the 21st century, evidence to suggest ongoing development of a local domestic architecture in New Zealand is sparse. Yet the belief that a uniquely and recognisably New Zealand house might exist was first established as a cultural discussion-point a hundred years ago on the cusp of the 20th century, when it hardly mattered that there was little physical evidence. However, by the 1940s, urged on by the centenary of the signing of the Treaty of

ABOVE LEFT All rooms act as viewing platforms for the wooded scenery. Privacy is achieved thanks to surrounding mature plantings and uneven land. Wooden shutters control sunlight here and adjustable glass louvres for air circulation feature throughout.

ABOVE The design concept began with an investigation of the relationship between a light wooden frame and solid retaining block walls and an ideal of creating a boathouse-like retreat within the city – as exemplified in this dining area.

RIGHT Semi-opaque glass provides visual contrast to the transparency of the house. Concertina doors to the deck open flush to expose the great outdoors. Entrance is via descending steps down the slope of the site to this courtyard, which also acts as a terrace.

Waitangi (which had brought peace between the Maori chiefs and the British crown) and the nationalism that tends to accompany wars, triggered by the onset of World War II, New Zealand architects began to pay more attention to the built manifestation of the "Kiwi" house. (My husband is a Kiwi, his father a property developer from Christchurch, so I do feel somewhat qualified to comment on their built environment.) The first example to achieve widespread acceptance as a typical style was a small house built during the summer of 1949 by Group Construction, later renamed Group Architects.

This was the first of many built in the late 1940s and the 1950s which led to establishment of the characteristics of the "typical" New Zealand house that have been applied since. The criteria (not an issue of style, more a democratic and egalitarian thrust) were that it should be modest in scale, innovative in its design and within affordable reach. Lastly, it should be made from wood, although true consideration for the environment came later. Eventually postwar "builders", probably perceiving timber as unsophisticated, disguised it behind wallboard or brick veneers. Architects, on the other hand, inclined to the experimental, exploring exposed timber as cladding, floorboards, wall-linings and ceilings. Latterly on the South Island, architects added other materials and adapted wood in recognition of climatic variation. By the 1970s, what had started out as a list of principles had resulted in a real style. In the late 1940s architecture had been tied to the ongoing affordability of timber, and pine forests planted during the Depression powered timber architecture well into the 1980s. Yet by the time the North Island's Clifford Forsyth House was completed, timber costs had escalated, and it may turn out to be one of the last houses of its type.

Architectus, one of New Zealand's pre-eminent contemporary architectural practices, has made a major contribution to the changing face of the New Zealand built environment. Started more than 20 years ago by Patrick Clifford (who graduated as an architect in 1981), Malcolm Bowes and Michael Thomson, Architectus has won just about every New Zealand Institute of Architects award for architecture, and many of their buildings have become New Zealand's modern architectural icons. Recently moving into the international arena, the practice has joined with a group of Australian architects to form offices elsewhere with connections to other practices around the world. Today Architectus brings together the experience of more than 160 leading architects, designers and planners, with offices in Auckland, Brisbane, Melbourne, Sydney and Shanghai.

Despite his very worthy accolades, and larger builds, Clifford remains a memorable house designer. I cannot help but wonder if in recent years the socialist ambitions of the original wooden-house designers have been subverted into the production of a new cultural product, the architect-designed house as a rich person's plaything – although not, of course, in the case of this house, with its rigorous structure and calmly unpretentious mood. In New Zealand, as in Australia, we continue to see a move from architectural egalitarianism to architectural elitism (note the shift of contemporary architecture from the suburb to the beach), and I only hope it is not a permanent one.

LEFT The units of the kitchen, which defines one side of the open-plan living/dining space, follow the angled wall.

BOTTOM FAR LEFT The frame and walls of the 250sq m (2,690sq ft) house sit on a concrete base, while a folded plate roof, underlined with plywood, tops it all off. The approach is from the street above.

BOTTOM CENTRE Use of wood can be modern. According to the architect, "environmental ethics means full understanding of the ecological interdependence of the development."

BOTTOM LEFT Generally for the past century the architect-designed New Zealand house has been wooden. Here ceiling joists are exposed and the staircase has an open-grille balustrade.

SKETCH The house has three storeys. The main floor is in the middle, with guest suites below and two bedrooms and a bathroom upstairs. Decks are cantilevered.

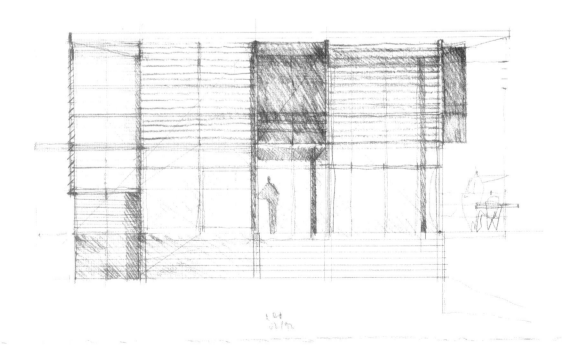

Forest lair
Embedded in a Johannesburg hillside, South African architect Johann Slee's home treats the surrounding forest as not only its garden but even part of the house, blurring the moment between inside and out. A solid cliff-like structure, it opens up like caves into the tree canopy. "The forest is a stage set," says the architect.

Unlike his European counterparts, Slee designs more residences than any other kind of building. In Europe, architects tend to survive through commercial projects and space is rare (helpful land and building laws rarer still). Twelve houses is the average per year in Johannesburg alone for Slee and his small team. The delightful "treehouse" he has built as his own home nestles in the forest in Westcliff, one of Johannesburg's oldest suburbs, and is paean to environmentally conscious building.

The plot, originally 0.4ha (1 acre), as are most in the area, has been reduced by half (the other half is let to another architect). The house, a labyrinth of corridors and rooms that billow at you on approach, was built upwards and downwards using the footprint of the previous, much smaller and humbler 1960s house, home of the illustrator who designed the South African currency, the rand, in 1961 when the South African pound was replaced by the newer currency to reflect the new republic's birth. Slee, an Afrikaner, rather enjoys knowing the previous place housed an artist since he paints too. Ever fond of history, he quips of South Africa, "The British built the roads and the Dutch built the houses.... Both were very good at it – the British created a good infrastructure and the Dutch added vision."

Moroccan modern

Karim El Achak is a modern architect, his Marrakech house a paean to good international architecture, by which I mean it can be understood by many cultures and would work well in any climate where the sun beats down. It is well thought out, cool in summer and a visual, colourful treat, yet without visual noise.

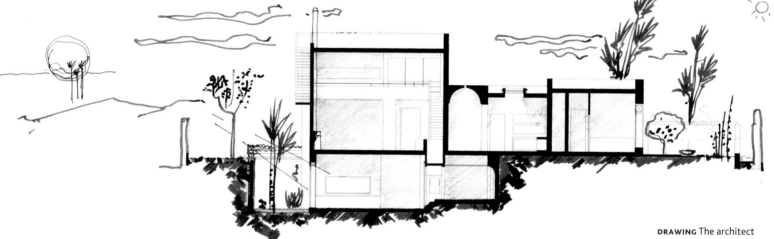

Morocco today is a very different scene from the 1960s hippy destination, with far more to offer than the sights and sounds of the kasbah, medina and bazaars. It is a journey today's hipsters are making with increasing frequency: tourism is up by 25 percent on average per year, and more and more outsiders are buying property since it offers good potential for growth.

Cosmopolitan Marrakech is the epicentre of the real-estate boom and it is not much of a surprise any longer to find world-class architects, local or imported, working in the region – and not just in the luxurious Palmeraie area inhabited mainly by French sophisticates. There are barren areas now under construction, including the as yet unsignposted location on the edge of the cultivated suburb of Palmeraie where architect Karim El Achak has elected to build his family home. For insiders and outsiders, the appeal of Morocco goes beyond investment potential. It is a wonderful place to live, and bring up children, and probably the most exotic country you can reach within a three-hour flight from many of Europe's cities; its unique decorative style, vibrant culture and warm year-round climate make it all the more appealing: Marrakech stays at around 20–21°C (about 68°F) in winter and has 300 days of sunshine; it is a dry heat so no problems sleeping at night.

I first came across the work of architect Karim El Achak at a small luxury development just outside Marrakech. A lovely, fertile spot surrounded by cypresses, orange and fig trees, it

DRAWING The architect has sketched his home in section to include its subterranean level. Subterranean living in a warm climate can only be successful in dry heat. Underground is a family room and an integral mosque, raised slightly. Note the depiction of the sun's movement.

RIGHT El Achak always builds around flora, then cultivates more. Palms in dusty Marrakech are often shifted at whim. His home, here the front, is built on an interesting configuration of axes.

FAR LEFT Pigmented exterior walls help to apportion the cultivated garden and block views of less-inspired houses. Marrakech is warm and sunny year-round. We photographed the house in autumn for blue sky: in summer the sky is white.

LEFT The rear of Villa Anjal is the most spectacular façade, huge glazed, metal-framed doors standing like sentries. The swimming pool is deeper by the house so a refreshing dive is achieved without a walk on hot stone. Terraces are local stone.

was full of birdsong and the scent of orange blossom. A true conservationist (of buildings and landscape), El Achak had insisted that most of the trees be preserved, despite the density of the building, and they now produce their own olives, olive oil and other goodies.

The second time I encountered his work, it was a riad refurbishment in Marrakech: the magnificently rich-looking yet minimalist chic Riad 72. Riads are traditional Moroccan buildings – a house set around a courtyard, with typical features including mosaics, Moorish arches and often a water feature.

I was delighted when I contacted El Achak for the first time to find he was in the process of completing his own home, which had taken two years to build. With true Moroccan hospitality he invited us to visit, but before we could set foot inside we shared tea and a hearty breakfast. In Morocco, houses seem more revered and people more polite than elsewhere.

Closely involved in the project has been El Achak's wife, an Italian Catholic, whom he met when studying architecture in Italy. They eventually married and returned to Marrakech, where they have been based for 15 years (their two young sons speak equally Italian and Arabic and not-at-all-bad English).

The architect, who is originally from Casablanca and has film-star looks, is quick to describe his work as "inspiring wellbeing" before slipping into the pool for a midday cool-down. The main house is airy and spacious, open on most sides (west only at subterranean level), since the Moroccan sun is so high in the sky that issues such as being "south-facing" simply do not apply. There is also a small single-storey traditional Moroccan-style guesthouse in a private plot behind a wall in the garden, its tiny mosaic bathrooms and kitchens reminiscent of riad living.

Entry to the main house, once you have passed the concealed guesthouse, is directly into the living room from the pathway. A lofty, predominantly white room, it has a mezzanine balcony that looks over the main room and has

RIGHT El Achak has created his own art using Moroccan trays. Other artwork, by a local artist, is created using sands of neighbouring regions. Door and window frames are black metal, which behaves well in the climate. Furniture is from Moroso, including a T-Phoenix powder-coated steel table by Patricia Urquiola.

typical blackened Moorish screens in the outside wall allowing limited light in and giving a view on the world beyond.

One seating arrangement is also traditional in that, built-in, it sweeps around the perimeter of a seating niche, its cushions padded for luxuriousness and vibrant in gem colours. Around the fireplace is a less traditional seating arrangement, a contemporary sofa and cantilevered tables.

The dining area, the focus of the house, is towards the back, and leads to a terrace and the garden. These contain more Italian contemporary furniture and chairs by award-winning designer Patricia Urquiola. "Being Moroccan doesn't preclude us from the high end of modern design," says the architect with a smile.

Bedrooms are in a separate wing on the ground floor and downstairs, at subterranean level, is a palatial office-cum-TV room and den, or "family room". Just beyond its casual seating is a door, up a couple of steps from floor level, which leads to El Achak's own personal mosque, an absolute treat for anyone's eyes but out of respect we do not show it here. The elegant and soft-spoken El Achak is a devout Muslim and is educating his children likewise.

Spending much of his time campaigning for responsible redevelopment of the city's historical sites, including a controversial project to conserve a marketplace due for demolition, he exhibits generosity and warmth at work and at home. It was a pleasure to visit. He even insisted I send a taxi to pick up my husband and baby from the hotel in Marrakech so he could extend his hospitality. Within a few minutes they too were keeping cool in the pool, which as we watched evaporated inches before our eyes!

OPPOSITE The main entrance is less grand than the rear. Floors are full ceramic porcelain stoneware. Although El Achak has used traditional wall effects such as *tadelak*, where shine is added to pigment, here walls have a modern powdery finish created by painting base onto chalk (only the bathrooms have *tadelak*). The stairs are concrete and red is used as accent colour. Rugs are Berber.

TOP LEFT Landscaping at the front of the house is as geometric as its interior and its footprint.

TOP CENTRE Italy-based Spanish designer Patricia Urquiola is a favourite of the couple: dining chairs are Bloomy by Urquiola for Moroso. Red comes to life in winter sunshine (whereas blue is luminous in dimness). As El Achak points out, "The sun does not enter the house at all in summer: the Moroccan sun is too high overhead." Double doors open inwards in French manner to bring in any breeze.

TOP RIGHT An outdoor shower peeks from behind a floating wall in the rear garden and a mature olive tree stands proud. Water is at a premium in the desert and a garden can be quite an undertaking. The poolside chairs are legless and ultra modern.

ABOVE El Achak's wife, Clara Candido, has a firm that produces handcrafted Moroccan objects for export. Her creative stamp is evident throughout: many fabrics and objects are pieces she has collated. The seating in this niche is a traditional element modernised. The ceiling, by contrast, is highly ornamental.

Vaulting ambition
Overlooking verdant vineyards and orchards near the Adriatic coast of central Italy, a former monastery has been transformed into a sympathetic home. Architect Paolo Badesco has unified an interior space so that it is primed for modern living yet has not lost its historical value and spirit.

Le Marche – touted as the "new Tuscany" – stretches inland from the beach resorts and ports of the Adriatic coastline. With its unspoilt beauty and excellent food and drink, it is the most mysterious of the triumvirate of regions that comprise central Italy (the others being Tuscany and Umbria), except for the weather, which is always balmy in summer and cool in winter – perfect for a seasonal retreat from city life.

If you plan to go to Le Marche (and you should – few visitors penetrate its hinterland) you need to sort out the pronunciation first. Le Marche is pronounced "lay markay". It translates into English as "the Marches" and that's how many of us know it. The scenery is frankly exquisite: approaching the coastal plain, mountains drop to gently rounded hills, often topped with fortified towns a millennium or more old, surrounded by green, fertile slopes of olive groves and vineyards. And then the land drops again to the long, broad, shallow beaches where there are excellent stretches of sand, and then the Conero peninsula, a rugged limestone promontory (limestone is a fantastic building material). As with much of Italy, wine is important to the region, and the classic wine of Marche is Verdicchio, a crisp, young, green-tinged white, excellent with fish and seafood – and since there is plenty of coast, there is plenty of seafood.

So it is no surprise that a canny couple of shoe designers from Milan might choose to have their summer home in Le Marche, far from the madding Tuscan crowds. No surprise also that they should choose a fellow Milanese, architect Paolo Badesco, to help with the restoration of their find.

As you leave the snaking road to the house, which through the vineyards appears as an austere rectangular form in red brick (Italian red brick is much paler than British), you soon become aware of the building's age. Mighty from the outside and demure from within, it was originally a 15th-century monastery, and like the countryside around it, has hidden secrets – not least the sweeping vaulted ceilings that lift and fall as if intonating the space. The staccato vaults, in their soldier uniformity, are almost audible,

BELOW LEFT In the kitchen, windowpanes are recessed directly into the curved wall without frames, for optimum pane area. Chairs are from Cappellini and the central workstation is stainless steel and Corian from Boffi.

BELOW The Milanese are beginning to choose Le Marche over Tuscany for second homes for peace and quiet. Milan-based architect Badesco was chosen to restore and refurbish the building in a contemporary but sensitive manner.

RIGHT Soft light pours under the low vaulted ceilings. Daylight also bounces off the white floor, almost lighting them up (in olden days the opposite would have been desired: the vaults would have remained dark and mysterious).

their tone softened visually by gentle light from the windows. "Intuitively he understood that the purity of the ceilings called for a rehabilitation that would be sober and contemporary," the owners say of Badesco's approach. The monastic element continues into the selection of tailored furniture and a neutral palette. This is a home for a family with young children, so stark minimalism was not going to work – but peace and serenity does.

The focus of the project was to completely re-cover all the interior surfaces of the house, to create a clean and fluid space, except for interior brickwork which was duly and dutifully washed. A main concern was the floor, which has been completely covered with a white resin containing marble dust that gives it depth and patina. The floor's uniformity gives the home a sense of continuity and visual flow, underlining the structure above.

The architect also "modernised" the house by reapportioning the volumes of the upstairs floor – there are now four substantial bedrooms and larger ultra-chic bathrooms. The parents' bedroom is very sober indeed, the children's more playful, but all have a tranquil spirit.

There are many successes in this very beautifully restored house but the true heroes are the vistas and views over the deeply undulating clipped countryside where vines and soft fruits grow in abundance. No surprise, therefore, that the kitchen, stuffed with homemade compotes of apricots picked just outside the door, offers prime views through large picture windows. In a region boasting such good food and wine, the kitchen cannot but be the hub of the home. Architecturally the room was a challenge to Badesco, who at first felt it was overly exposed to the elements. The central unit brought the space together (there were no free walls once windows were in place) and the kitchen has now found its identity. This is a time for inspiration in the region, for inserting modernity into ancient, working with extreme features – even exaggerating them – and unifying the rest.

ABOVE Clinton Murray's "green" awareness has meant his signatures generally include excellent orientation and cross-ventilation (no air conditioning), as well as energy-efficient concrete floors that function as thermal mass, conserving heat. Here you can see right through the house.

LEFT The back of the house, or rather the approach, has been landscaped into the hillside. The woodenness of the building is most evident here: its cladding will change with time, and some wood weathers beautifully. Clinton, who believes in hands-on involvement, worked closely with his group of three carpenters.

Murray, who has been described in the Australian press as "intense and irreverent", is a likeable fellow and there is something about this Australian architect's work that falls into similar vein to that of the cherished American architect Charles Gwathmey. Since I am extremely fond of the smaller projects Gwathmey presented in the 1960s and 1970s – the wooden Cubist house built for his parents in Amagansett on Long Island in particular – I am not really surprised I find Clinton Murray's new build here in Merimbula appealing.

For the Tasman House, Murray anchored the L-shaped home around the pool and deck, central to the main wing of the house facing the sea. To the rear of the house, which inclines upwards onto a hill to the north, is a garage. From this, you enter the house from the rear through an entry court and immediately have the southerly view over the Tasman Sea. This is the upper level, where guest rooms and a study make up the corner of the building; to the east, beyond the central deck, there is an open-plan living-cum-dining room and, further towards the end of the house, a kitchen.

Downstairs, accessible from a central staircase, the footprint of the house is much the same, anchored by the deck at this level and the over-lengthy pool spilling out towards the sea. Of the sea the architect says, "You can almost fall into it – or dive into the pool." Beneath the garage are storerooms, while at the corner of the building on this lower level are the three children's bedrooms built in strict uniformity (three in a row) and their trapezium-shaped playroom. The master-bedroom suite is directly underneath the living and dining room at the eastern end of the house.

Ostensibly a wooden structure with vast windows front and back, the house is made breezy by louvred glass window panels – possibly its most 1970s inflection. It was built with a team of three carpenters, Ty Simpson, David Gardener and Don O'Connell, with Alan Simpson heading up the building team. The landscaping is by Clinton's brother Andrew Murray.

Gwathmey's work has been described, by the great architect Robert A. M. Stern, as rising "from vernacular roots to the lyricism of high art" and "liberated from the constraints of the prevailing modernism". I believe Clinton Murray's work will similarly continue to impress for its rigour and its clarity, for its movement away from current tastes and for the fact that he builds in response to human functions and dimensions, with respect for economy of means.

ABOVE Inside, sliding doors help to reapportion the rooms. The interior space has a seamless flow despite the fact that there are many functional elements to the house, home to a family with three children. Ease and efficiency was a must.

BELOW & BELOW RIGHT Murray anchored the house around the pool and deck, which are central to the main wing of the building, facing the sea (the house forms an L shape). When you are in the pool you can swim right into the belly of the structure.

ABOVE At the western corner of the building on the lower level are the three regimented children's bedrooms and their trapezium-shaped playroom. Above them are guest rooms and study. The house is a permanent home, not a holiday extravaganza. It is inhabited all year round.

ABOVE RIGHT This end of the building houses the living-cum-dining room on the upper level and, beneath it, the master-bedroom suite.

PLAN The L-shaped house is clearly defined by the floor plan (here showing the lower level), with the pool jutting out perpendicular to the principal wing. The landscaping was very relevant to the position of the build, although the view and sea orientation took precedence over all aspects in the final plan.

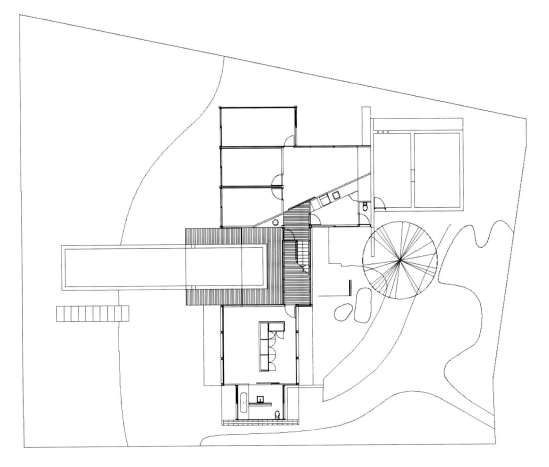

hillside

Living on a hill is akin to sitting in a tall-backed chair. It makes you feel more important – as if you are at the top of your ladder, so to speak. As Alfred, Lord Tennyson wrote, "Live and Lie reclined on the hills like Gods together, careless of mankind. For they lie beside their nectar and the bolts are hurled far below them in the valleys, and the clouds are lightly curled round their golden houses, girdled with the gleaming world."

Besides any psychological advantage, living on a hill brings its own climatic benefits. For accurate assessment of climate, several factors that influence temperature and precipitation must be taken into account: not only the obvious question of latitude – which determines the angle of the sun's rays and hence the intensity of solar energy received – but also variables such as elevation (alternatively referred to as altitude), prevailing wind direction and topography. Elevation is the height above sea level. As you go higher up a mountain, the air pressure decreases and its molecules spread farther and farther apart. Less dense air is cooler than dense air, so the farther above sea level you are, the lower the temperature will be.

Furthermore, being on a hill generally means you are exposed to flowing air, with all the cooling benefits a breeze can bring in a hot climate. The precise impact will depend on whether you are on the windward or leeward side of the hill in terms of prevailing winds, and on details of local topography, which will serve to channel airflow. These issues must be thoroughly considered when siting and orientating a building. The Southern African house revealed in this chapter was built atop a hill overlooking a lake; it is hot up there, but the cool breeze even makes it conceivable to play tennis – at least at certain times of the day.

Less dense air can hold less water, so as air rises over mountains it deposits any excess water molecules it is carrying as rain (or snow, in conditions where the temperature is cold enough). If the prevailing winds bring air that has just travelled over water, it will be carrying a great deal of moisture, which will fall on the windward side of the mountains; by the time the air reaches the leeward side it will be largely rained out, and the leeward side will be left in a rain shadow, much drier – another factor to consider in choosing a site.

Shade is also an issue. Being on a hot hilltop brings the risk of over-exposure to the sun, but if you use the shading of the hill well, choosing the right side and taking advantage of natural irregularities, you can make the topography work in your favour. Again, this requires careful planning, just as the legendary 20th-century designer Eileen Gray spent a year viewing her plot at Roquebrune in the south of France from all angles and in all weathers and moods before building there.

Building on a hill must be clever, perhaps curving around the hillside or creating intricate shapes that allow three-dimensional movement up and down as well as to and fro within the building as conditions of sun and wind change according to the time of day or night. The Ibiza house featured in this chapter is closed on one side and opens up to the sea on the other, thereby directing its use.

A further challenge is simply to transport the necessary materials up to the site. In the case of an ambitious project, it can literally take years to complete a building. But, as all three of these examples show, it is worth it simply for the impact of the site, the views, the sense of living like a god.

OPPOSITE The predominantly glass house designed by Helena Arahuete of Lautner Associates is located on the South Sister of the Twin Sisters in Napa, California, with an elevation of 689m (2,259ft). Views are magnificent.

Hilltop eyrie
Perched on a Napa hilltop above the vineyards, this superlative example of California architecture by Helena Arhuete, with its window walls and magnificent views, brings together birdlike grace and sophisticated engineering. This is what living on top of the world is about: using 21st-century skills to make the most of an elevated location and create a home where you can really breathe.

Up until now I have held close to my heart the house I think is one of the most spectacular in the world. It was for sale again at the very end of the 20th century for an awful lot of money, and I could only dream of owning it. The architect, the late John Lautner, designed (with an interior by someone else whose work I admire wholeheartedly, the late Michael Taylor) a magnificent oceanfront house on a rocky promontory at La Chuza Point in Malibu, its baying glass windows giving view to rough waters beneath. The interior incorporated natural elements – huge riverbed boulders, for example, to break up the geometry of the architecture inside, as well as Taylor's fantastic scheme of spherical white

ABOVE Sloping roofs, high from the outside but low on the interior courtyard side, capture the vistas and visually pull them towards the house. Angular rooflines echo the forms of the distant mountains. The upper level is 90 percent glass in 4.5m (15ft) panels.

BELOW On the south side is a 15m (50ft) indoor/outdoor lap pool. Dividing glass panels over it slide aside on motorised overhead tracks. Its supporting beam tapers, lessening apparent heftiness with a grace typical of Arhuete. Chairs are Summit.

The decks are slate-covered in true Lautner style; concrete and slate stairs lead to the house entrance. The combination of materials – fir, mahogany (inside), concrete and glass – makes for a truly harmonious vision at one with the surroundings.

ABOVE In the centre of the house is the two-storey courtyard. Despite being surrounded by 688ha (1,700 acres) of wooded landscape, the couple decided to contain their own portion of the outdoors within the six-sided house. The courtyard remains cool.

ABOVE RIGHT : Ceilings are clad in vertical-grain Douglas fir and pitch and sweep, dipping down to 2m (7ft) over built-in sofas, rising to 4.5m (15ft) at the tallest windows. The interior design was aided by Siobhan Brennan of John Wheatman & Associates.

cushions and oversized puffy white sofas. It symbolises utterly the California dream. Built in 1983, the floors are slabs of slate in almost free form: Lautner had held firm the naturalistic ideals of his teacher, the great Frank Lloyd Wright, but had developed a style all of his own, using glass instead of brick, and local slates and stone.

So when Helena Arahuete, who had worked with Lautner from 1971 until his death in 1994, continued to practise using the Lautner name, I have to say I was a little sceptical and doubted that anything quite as magnificent could ever be created in the name of Lautner again.

I was wrong. This project, completed in 2004 (it was first conceived of in 1998) by Arahuete with Lautner Associates for client John Roscoe, is a superlative example of fine California architecture with its window walls and magnificent views, and quite evidently continues the spirit of Lautner without being pastiche. The Roscoe residence, in Napa, positioned at the very apex of the hill, looks as if it is about to take off yet is not at odds with the vineyard surroundings. It is splendid on approach and splendid within, and has a grace I have not seen in residential architecture in years. As with the old Lautner, there has to be one amazing fanfare moment and here it is the pool, which transgresses from house to exterior so you can actually swim from inside to out. When the windows slide over at night, or when there is cooler weather, it is possible to swim underneath the glass: a remarkable building feat, and moreover a good idea.

A home's surroundings always pitch the house itself, or should do, and this residence is surrounded by a panorama of sky. Glass houses have often beguiled architects: glass is solid yet invisible, present yet transparent. What Arahuete has done is to create an Expressionistic vision, with what appear to be vast shards of glass exploding into the air. The house gives

ABOVE Arahuete has created her own signature detail in the *faux bois* concrete design on some interior walls. The owners insisted that all fireplaces should be at floor level, no raised hearths.

RIGHT The pool enters the house near breakfast and dining areas separated by a fireplace. The house is composed of expansive spaces, with unobstructed views from every room on the main floor.

LEFT With all its wood, the house has a fire-retardent metal roof. A prerequisite was to be able to cool it down to 23°C (72°F) on hot days, but nights can be cold.

TOP The kitchen has been kept to a minimum, functional and slick. Slate floors throughout give visual continuity.

ABOVE Exterior steps lead from upper floor to lower within the courtyard. This house is far from sedentary, with numerous passageways.

PLAN The massive interior space of 1,254sq m (13,500sq ft) has a steel-beamed roof. The plan of the house shows its originality and ingenuity.

views stretching from San Francisco's Golden Gate Bridge on one horizon to the Sierra Nevada on the other. The hills of Napa's wine country roll beneath.

Owners John and Marilyn Roscoe loved hiking in these hills, so they slowly purchased adjoining parcels of land, gathering 688ha (1,700 acres) including two sugar-loaf peaks, the Twin Sisters, that command the immediate area. Roscoe's remit was to give everything to the 360-degree view, and Belgian-born Arahuete, who was raised in Argentina, another country with big landscape, produced unobstructed views from every room on the main floor; even from the kitchen the vista is filled with the Twin Sister peak to the north. As Arahuete says, "The views are a constant presence."

The structure is stern: built of concrete poured in place, it has a steel-beam roof yet its main floor seems to float lithely above the ground, while its terraces jut out into space. The geometry, stylistically speaking, is not as complicated as it first seems and, despite its angles and the fact that "the perspective of each angle changes as you move", as the architect points out, it cannot be dubbed "de-constructed" as could the more complicated architecture fad of the moment (think Daniel Libeskind and Zaha Hadid). Construction was, however, challenging, and Arahuete was assisted for some elements — for example the pool, which cantilevers over the sloping hillside despite its weight — by Andrew Nasser, the engineer who structured some of Lautner's most challenging designs.

The house, 1,254sq m (13,500sq ft) of interior floor space, has intimate and grander moments, and privacy is still possible within (glass houses have been criticised non-stop for their goldfish-bowl characteristics), not just because of the remoteness of the location but also thanks to the design. This is achieved even when there are guests, as there often are, once three hundred at once. The main space consists of kitchen and dining, living and pool rooms. "We all have simple needs, really," says Roscoe. Downstairs, sunk into the hillside a little, are a library, utility rooms, exercise rooms and two guest rooms.

As Lautner learned from Frank Lloyd Wright, Arahuete has learned from John Lautner. A magnificent 21st-century *oeuvre* has already been built. In John Roscoe's words, "We are very pleased with the house designed by Helena Arahuete and very pleased with the house that has been constructed. We realise and appreciate the great effort expended by those who strove valiantly to overcome the difficulties inherent in the project."

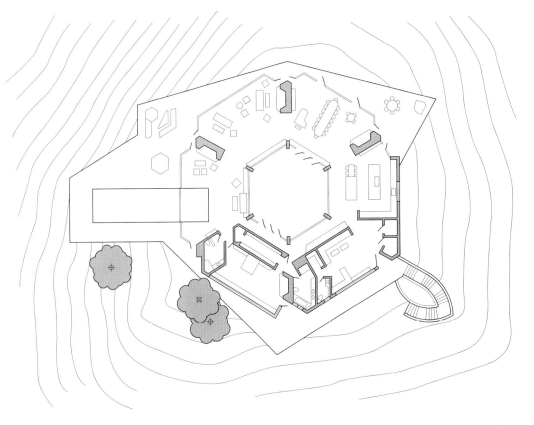

Little boxes on the hillside Casa Na Xemena, the house built
by architect Ramón Esteve in the remote landscape of the hamlet of Na Xemena
for client José Gandia, takes prime place on Ibiza's glorious craggy north coast and
looks out upon absolute nothingness but sea and sky horizon: the house is silent.

Enclosed at the rear, the south side, the house remains as cool as a cucumber despite the raging sun, which, at times in the Balearics, seems unstoppable. As a teenager I holidayed in the Balearics on occasion and thinking back, I believe the reason we imagine the climate is really hot is because we go there to vacation. In Marrakech, where the outside temperature is hotter, and the arid desert dust drifts into our lungs, the fact that the city is a working hub makes the heat seem more palatable. In Cairo and Giza too, the climate can be almost too much at times, but we cope with it because we are busy sightseeing and thus perhaps equip ourselves better. Ibiza, on the other hand, has no business, just relaxation, and that is when we feel it the most: up for a swim, a light breakfast, a book by the pool, lunch and finally a sundowner on the terrace – it is all about the heat and, quite frankly, we soak it up it, as long as we can find refuge inside.

Originally one small, box-like *finca* or cottage, Casa Na Xemena has been extended to a veritable *enfilade* of *finca*s, all open-plan inside and linked together with little interior upset except for the odd floor-level change. The house belongs to José Gandia of Gandia Blasco, a Spanish furniture firm which dates back to the 1940s and is best known for its outdoor and lighting products. It is his second home and he rarely comes alone: guest rooms are abundant, six with *en suite* bathrooms, and room for more. The guest suites are moulded into the form of the house under the main level so it is difficult to see them from either front or back.

BELOW Casa Na Xemena, high on the craggy north coast of Ibiza, is a spectacular example of coherent and sequential design: from the rear the boxes comprising the house appear uniform, but the sea-facing view gives an understanding of the many levels.

RIGHT The infinity pool has been designed to run along two axes, across the front of the *enfilade* of box-like forms, and then to stretch out towards the Mediterranean on the north side of the island.

FAR LEFT Bathed in light, the white building pays homage to the domestic architecture of the Balearics. From the rear Moorish undertones are evident, quite a common sight in many Spanish regions. A common finish, white reflects both light and heat.

LEFT The architect has added many refuges from the elements such as terraces that fall into semi-shade at certain times of day according to the position of the sun in the sky. Rigid overhead sunshades are permanent and static.

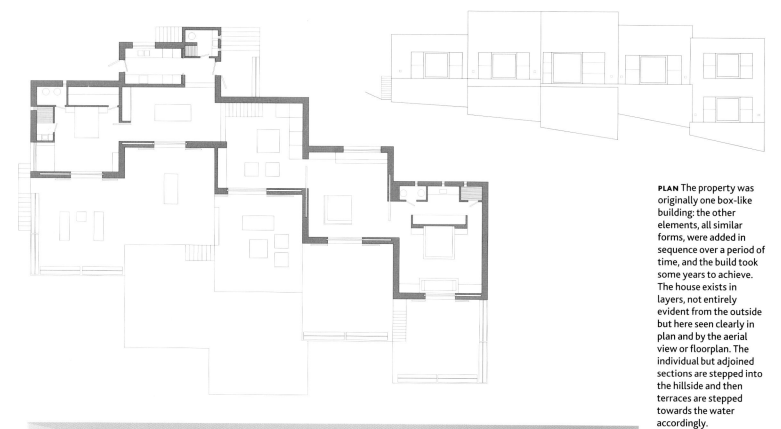

PLAN The property was originally one box-like building: the other elements, all similar forms, were added in sequence over a period of time, and the build took some years to achieve. The house exists in layers, not entirely evident from the outside but here seen clearly in plan and by the aerial view or floorplan. The individual but adjoined sections are stepped into the hillside and then terraces are stepped towards the water accordingly.

LEFT Iroko wood frames a huge picture window in a bedroom. Outdoor and indoor furniture was made specially for the house by Esteve but is now available though the owner's furniture firm. Sunken and raised baths in bedroom suites differ in size and form but are on the whole concrete.

RIGHT A shaft of light from an oblong window hits cantilevered stairs made from iroko wood, and is echoed by a suspended light. Seating is inbuilt and calico-covered for cool comfort.

LEFT The cobalt blue of the dining room helps delineate the rest of the white space. A bedroom and bathroom at the top of these stairs are encased in a wooden box. Entry to the house is into the dining room (via the steps seen here against the blue wall).

TOP The window in this bathroom area is a slit between two solid grey structures, the bath sunken. Greyness and texture separate the area from the bedroom, although it is very much within the room.

ABOVE A couple of steps help the "layering" of a simple building and add contemporary character. Iroko is used for ceilings and staircase as well as the kitchen, a minute space that indicates barbecues are the norm.

ABOVE RIGHT The bedroom in the wooden box has a low ceiling and is almost clinical in its simplicity. In a warm environment clutter can be stifling. Resin floors are durable, soft to touch, not too cold and easy to clean. Bedding is cotton or linen.

The front, the sea side, facing north away from the sun, is completely open, box-by-box, its infinity pool and terrace just edging onto the rocky hillside and the view beneath. The hill certainly invites a breeze onto the terrace and directly into the house, so much so that hanging lampshades swing gently just to remind us there is some kind of activity out there, life is not extinct. From the other sides, a spattering of small square and oblong perforations in the structure create theatrical lights inside the house by day, and at night beam spots of warm light onto the terrace outside.

Inside, powdery white and cobalt- and indigo-blue-pigmented walls create a thread running through the home, as do floors in grey tones, in almost Cubist manner. Iroko wood, an African hardwood also called Nigerian teak, which is hard and durable in humid climates, is used throughout, for ceilings and staircase as well as the kitchen (whose tiny size suggests that most cooking takes place outdoors). Iroko also frames three huge picture windows – reminiscent of the Groupe 7 house on Capri, also on a rocky coast overlooking water – giving dramatic sea views. Moving from box to box inside the house is seamless and the openings vast: there are no interior doors between the five elements.

The house has been an ongoing project for six years; the final two cube buildings have just been added to the three built in succession before. Somewhat removed from a formally planned geometric scheme, the slow pace of building has resulted in a collection of spaces that is articulated with a natural grace only time can bring.

When the house project began, Gandia Blasco was selling only textiles, but the building of Na Xemena encouraged a furniture collection. "The house dictated the pieces," says architect Esteve from his studio in Valencia. "The building was asking for furniture that was not on the market." The pieces, a neutral style of furniture that can adapt to many settings, have become a staple part of the firm.

Ramón Esteve graduated from the Architecture Superior Technique School of Madrid in 1990 and founded his own studio, realising several works in Spain from houses to larger commercial projects. Working also in interior and industrial design, he has received prizes for furniture, some of it for Gandia Blasco. Despite the kudos this house has given him, Esteve plans to continue designing commercially, in part because he doesn't like the tendency to make a statement with each individual work. He likes, in every sense, to just blend in.

The architect describes this house as "simple," since the five concrete cubes exhibit a premeditative linking of the topography, the architectonic set integrating into the landscape as it scales the rocky cliff. As he points out, "The main characteristic of the home is its isolation." This is highlighted by the cube form and the metal-framed sunshade, which seems to give the house a border.

View House

"We created a hilltop bastion-type sandstone structure, growing out of the prehistoric dune and topped with a wide-brimmed floating roof," says architect Johann Slee of his achievement. View House is a holiday home on the picturesque south coast of South Africa, a project where just sandstone, glass and wood have been used to create a very specific atmosphere; the house is at once peaceful and majestic, monastic yet suitable for a party.

On the top of a hill in Sedgefield, near Knysna, on the coastal road towards Plettenberg Bay, the client – from Holland – bought one of the most breathtaking views in the country and commissioned Slee to build him a holiday compound for his family, who are scattered around the globe. The site, unparalleled in beauty over any location I have set eyes upon (but then I love South Africa), is a prehistoric sand dune overlooking the Swartvlei estuaries.

From the winding hillside approach road, which begins near a railway line and ends what seems kilometres away at the pinnacle, the fortress looms large, apparently on the very edge of the hill. Despite the natural flora surrounding the house, there is still a rather large private garden (tennis courts too, but these are to be avoided in midday sun); the approach is through the garden and entry from the rear.

Enormous double reclaimed doors lead to a monastic interior courtyard which contains a square pond with simple drip fountain. It is used for quiet reflection and meditation, and there is only a wooden bench as furniture, plus one or two enormous pots. "Our architectural palette has its origins in the earth – muted earth colours, textured finishes reflecting abundant sunlight. Our built structures reflect simplicity and honesty, echoing the vernacular of local built forms. The beauty of detail is in the crude simplicity," says the architect.

The structure and its courts give refuge from the harsh elements but also open up to allow enjoyment of the exterior spaces and spectacular views in panorama. Through the doors opposite the initial entrance is the large rectangular "great hall", not unlike a medieval banqueting hall, which leads

TOP LEFT The lo-tech materials used for the fortress-like structure were simply local stone, wood and glass.

TOP RIGHT From the road beyond the railway you can see the bastion right at the hill's apex, its roofs alive in the sun.

ABOVE CENTRE The four main elements, one on each corner around a courtyard, suggest a medieval castle.

ABOVE On the east viewing platform Slee has built a "floating fire ring" for heat and *braais*, as barbecues are known.

THIS PAGE The disappearing edge pool melts into the lagoon on the west towards the estuary, giving from the main floor of the house. From the front double doors – huge imposing wooden structures – you can see through the courtyard with its meditation pool, into the main hall, not unlike a "great hall" of old, through to the deck and pool. It is one continuum. The upper level of the main floor also falls into a terrace overlooking the estuary.

All bedrooms are interior-designed simply, each one completely differently furnished with local artefacts or *objets trouvés*. No bed is the same as another. Linens and fabrics are generally local although some delightful pieces are European. Floors are stone.

RIGHT This is the inner courtyard, built for contemplation with its serene pool feature.

FAR RIGHT Each bedroom has its own bathroom – almost a prerequisite in a hot climate, bathing being so central to comfort (privacy and escape is another important factor). It does seem very un-European to bathe with a view but I think it a great luxury.

PLAN In aerial view the form is clear: public rooms are in the central section with the pool, private at the edges.

out to the terrace and the swimming pool, the latter overhanging the water. Above the swimming pool on the next level a sun deck has been built, also hanging out from the structure, giving a view over the pool beneath and the estuary and hills beyond.

At all four corners of the principal building stand fortress-like towers, each with a spiral stone staircase leading to quaint bedrooms and minimalist bathrooms. The bedrooms, on ground and upper levels, are individually designed, with unique pieces of African and antique furniture, and both bedrooms and bathrooms have enormous windows giving splendid views at every opportunity. Although the house design can accommodate extremely large family gatherings, these tower bedrooms are a retreat far from the madding crowd.

"We create space to live in. Our expertise lies in residential spaces, holiday homes and lodges, and selective commercial work that falls into our design philosophy," says the architect. Slee & Co is a multi-disciplined architecture and design practice with offices in Johannesburg (see pages 41–3 for Slee's own Johannesburg home) and Knysna. Having been an architect since the 1980s, Slee believes "South Africa is alive with possibility" for its room to build and its different vernaculars throughout the vast land – and for the talent too. "The philosophy behind our design is

to incorporate and respect the diverse aspirations and heritages of our clients; to learn from advanced technologies and to create a vernacular architecture, embracing our unique people, skills, climate and space," the architect explains.

One of Slee's projects, in his home town of Johannesburg in 2005, won *South African House and Leisure* magazine's "House of the Year" competition, in a country where new building is abundant. His design of the Red House, another recent residential project, was selected as winner in 2004 of the Residential Built Project category in the prestigious Cityscape Architectural Review Awards in Dubai, where all entries came from developing countries and judging criteria were based upon the design's contribution to world architectural culture, invention, imagination, environmental awareness and appropriateness. Wherever Slee builds in his vast country he uses indigenous materials and local stone, yet his designs travel well – they could be adapted to suit many hot terrains.

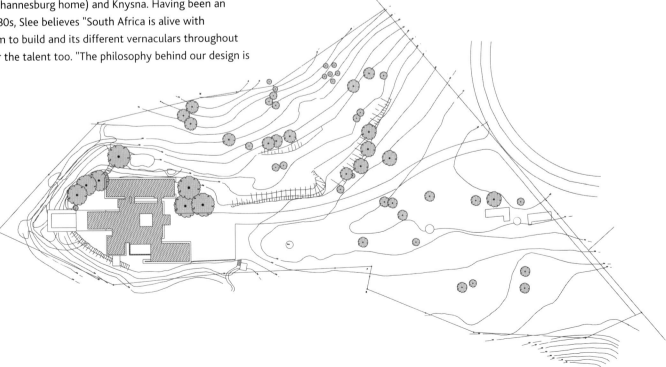

streetside

Cities create their own microclimates. Whatever climatic belt it is in, an urban area will always be a few degrees warmer than its surroundings, thanks to the heat exuded by its buildings and inhabitants, along with the effects of traffic. Buildings absorb the sun's heat by day and give it off at night, as well as generating heat themselves via their heating or cooling systems. They also create local winds, funnelling air flows down channels between structures. As a result of such factors, cloud cover and precipitation over cities will usually also differ markedly from surrounding regions. The effect of all this is that – without even starting to take into account the impact of pollution – the climatic problems of hot-climate living are exacerbated in a city.

The other key influence on an urban home is that mostly space is at a premium. This may radically cut back the options for combatting the elements – some just do require space in which to spread out – and it will no doubt mean that neighbours are nearby and, even if their homes do not physically block the ideal build, there will at least be psychological, aesthetic or legislative constraints on architectural expression (although these can serve to stimulate inventiveness).

Orientation, for instance, is a given: you have to face the street. Even if it would better meet light and shade requirements to site the house at an angle, there is rarely the choice – unless you are highly innovative and come up with a clever scheme such as shifting the axis of the building so that it meets all criteria (see pages 108–11). This kind of non-conformist thinking and hard work are required on many counts, to deal with sorting out air flows and cool spots as well as the more standard challenges.

Assuming building permissions and local authorities cannot be negotiated, the result may be a compromise on exterior design and a focus instead on the interior – although not in these examples, where the challenge has been met. A possible approach to urban design is to retain parts of an existing building and add new elements to it – a completely new build is a relative rarity – in which case we usually attempt to highlight what is worth preserving historically; in London this tends to mean Georgian, in Chicago or Los Angeles 20th-century. Such principles may seem restrictive but they can be food for inspiration too.

In non-urban hot environments, outdoor living is fundamental to coping with the heat, to the extent that divisions between indoor and outdoor often blur. But in a city, spending all day in the garden is frequently unviable: the house may have no garden or other outdoor space, and even if it does, issues of privacy and noise may discourage its use. Shaded balconies and roof terraces, up above prying eyes and the worst of the noise and pollution, and perhaps equipped with simple yet effective wood or rattan-type screens, thus come into their own as outdoor rooms. Similarly, and especially in newly designed homes, huge picture windows may be employed, although these must be carefully thought out so that they fulfil their objective of providing an almost-outdoor room without the noise or pollution but do not bring the oven effect of a greenhouse or any significant loss of privacy.

Architects working in a city may not be able to let their imaginations soar as they might elsewhere, but they do have to stretch their creative thinking to find solutions to often more complex problems if they are to achieve climate-sensitive urban design and provide people with a comfortable thermal environment. And at least city builds are easier in one respect: amenities are always close at hand.

OPPOSITE The Wrap House in Melbourne, Australia, spearheaded by Simon Knott, is constructed from rendered blockwork on a steel-portal frame and, unconventionally but correctly, faces sideways towards the north so the sun is easily controlled. A 9,000-litre (2,400-gallon) water-storage tank is located in the basement car garage to allow water reticulation to the garden and lawns.

Boxing clever Wrap House, winner of the Australian Design Awards Interior Design Selection 2004, was built for a semi-retired couple in a rather genteel Melbourne suburb, Toorak, previously better known for its red-tile roofs, brick-veneer cladding and disregard for orientation than for modernistic vision.

The house's architects were the firm BKK (Black Kosloff Knott), spearheaded by Simon Knott. All three directors of the firm, founded in 2000, are practising architects – Tim Black, Julian Kosloff and Simon Knott – and at least one of them is always closely involved in any project taken on, "to ensure the appropriate placement of resources and to take maximum advantage of the depth of skills" available within the office. Highly academic in their study and execution of their work, the trio claim to be actively involved in the local culture of design (after all, architecture does not happen in a vacuum), annually curating the "Lite" exhibition as part of the worldwide *Faites de la Lumière* celebration of creating light. All have been university educators in both architectural design and technology at RMIT (Royal Melbourne Institute of Technology) and maintain roles

OPPOSITE, TOP The house was sited to minimise excavation and use existing levels. A simple steel portal frame fixed to a suspended concrete slab was infilled with panels of concrete block and timber stud, and rendered over.

OPPOISTE, BOTTOM Environmentally, the house incorporates a number of energy-saving techniques. It was pushed to the southern edge of the site to maximise the northern solar aspect and connect living and external space.

THIS PAGE In the living area, materials were selected on the basis of finish, such as render, laminate and concrete floors requiring little maintenance. Concrete block and concrete screed floors were utilised for insulation.

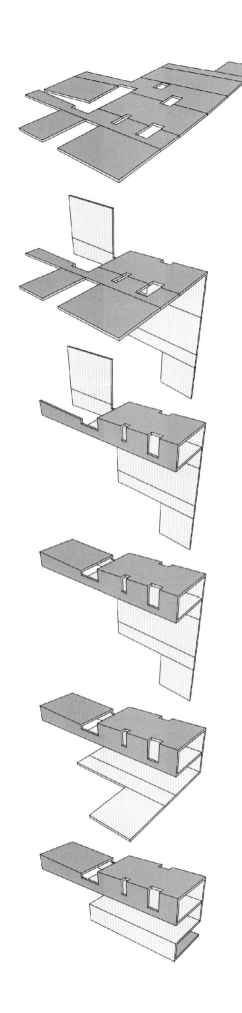

with the Royal Australian Institute of Architects. An award-winning firm, BKK's high-profile design projects have included commercial, institutional, retail, residential and governmental builds.

This kind of resumé, the scholarly kind, let me tell you as a "veteran" architecture writer (I was not entirely amused by this so-called accolade which appeared in print recently since it makes me sound ancient), is impressive but often makes my eyes roll, and I have to take a deep breath before even beginning to unravel the kind of work such highly esteemed architects are up to. How can I explain without upsetting people? Wholly academic firms, or those who practise from the philosophical standpoint – or those who are too pure in their do-gooding or at least sound as if they are – often produce work that somehow manages to evade the interest of the general public, except for some of the true talents of our times such as Zaha Hadid. Sometimes the work is so "architectural" it is impossible to see its merit without reading the subtext. On occasion only other architects quite see the point. I see a lot of this kind of work at the colleges, where quite frankly I am not surprised they go into such depth of study – after all, it takes longer to qualify as an architect than as a doctor. But in the real world, the holier-than-thou approach can be a little off-putting, "good" as it is meant to be. I am aware that architects have to study long and hard to be able to secure our safety, to study the laws and bylaws of the land and learn how to build magnificent *oeuvres* while learning about the more fundamental elements such as water-cooling systems and air conditioning, but I am not sure the outside world needs this much information. When I need a doctor, I want a diagnosis and prognosis, and that is about it – no deep discussion about cell counts and haemoglobin levels. Well, with architecture it's the same. How does it look and how does it feel and will it last long, stylistically and otherwise, are my first, and often only, questions.

It is therefore thrilling when looking at and experiencing the work of BKK, particularly the Wrap House in the Melbourne suburbs, that they have, fortunately, simply built a fantastic house. You don't need the subtext to realise how fantastic the house actually is – although it is relevant to know that the firm's design methodology "focuses on a response to both occupant and site, providing a solution that shies away from the merely fashionable aspects of contemporary design," hoorah!

It is true that the architects make much of the notion of wrap, a proposition about how architecture might approach from other directions than customary orientation and structure. It is suggested by BKK that the design for the Wrap House comes from a sequence of folds in a carefully cut flat sheet. In a way, the wrap hardly matters, for here is a series of dramatic domestic spaces light years beyond the imagination of the builders of the surrounding brick-tile mini-mansions. "There is little or no resemblance to the traditional spatiality of a house with long corridors and a sequential layout of rooms. Rather, a progression through the house is highly modulated. Spaces flow from one to the next and are largely differentiated by their height and volume," comments architect Simon Knott. In fact the expression does not seem particularly to relate to the way the rooms are arranged inside, only impacting on the ground-floor library and upper-floor master bedroom, which both have large picture windows exposed to the fierce westerly sun in the afternoons; I imagine the picture windows are there for formal reasons to complete the wrap, and they do have integral sun blinds.

According to the clients, the architects have bestowed upon them everything they wanted; the steep approach from street up to the house's ground-floor level was a given, due to the steeply sloping site, something the architects had to work with and not at all their fault. In the final analysis, this might be "clever" architecture but it is good architecture and moreover a very sound home.

PLAN The house's flatpack-like flattened plane is folded around internal service blocks, "shaping" the interior space by providing an envelope. The Wrap House presents a number of differentiated and varied volumes.

RIGHT, ABOVE Highlight colours are chosen to add points of reference and draw the interior through to the lush landscaping. The banding to the exterior render is carried though to the internal face by alternating bands of gloss and matt paint.

RIGHT At the upper level, the elevation reads as a series of solid blocks separated by glazing. Large picture windows grace the master bedroom, which faces the street and the fierce afternoon sun. The sun blinds also offer privacy.

FAR RIGHT Concrete block, render, plasterboard and metal deck are the simple infill materials that complete the fabric of the house. Through economic detailing and selection the interior fit-out is a cost-effective solution.

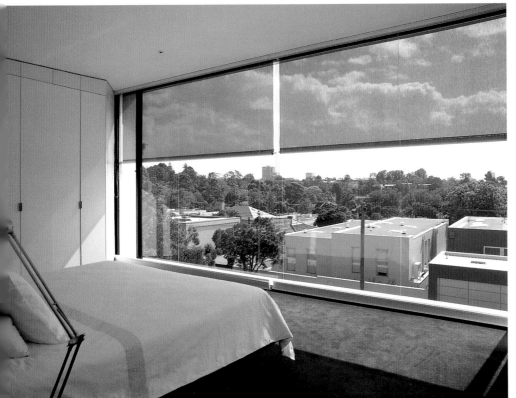

CASE STUDY

Fabric of invention

Steven Ehrlich is an urban architect, if ever there was one, for his values and principles. But while he works at the forefront of new technology, he is also influenced by the courtyards and souks of African architecture, especially of Morocco and Nigeria. The results are evident in the verging-on-industrial yet caravanserai-like home he has built for himself and his wife on a narrow corner plot in Venice, Los Angeles.

Ehrlich sees himself as an "architectural anthropologist", understanding connections between "architecture and culture, people and place". Founded in 1979, his award-winning Steven Ehrlich Architects (SEA) is a 20-strong sole proprietorship based in Culver City, California. Here he finds himself happily in the vanguard of technological advancement and the truly modern world with all its lively trappings, and with a little more space to work than architects in the cramped conditions of Cairo or Mexico City, for instance in his "high-tech high-touch" environment, a 5.2ha (13-acre) plot designed for DreamWorks for their one-thousand-strong creative workforce.

Apart from successful designs for lofts in Venice Beach and his pending "Multi-Family" housing project at City Place in Santa Ana, Ehrlich has also

ABOVE LEFT The vista on entry to the house sweeps right through and out the other side. Crazy paving is a quirky addition but right at home in the hustle and bustle that is Venice, LA.

ABOVE To one side of the main living space is a smaller room for television and reading. A modern home need not be a bare home: here books are neatly housed in floor-to-ceiling bookshelves.

RIGHT A 5m- (16ft) tall window wall slides open to the sculptural trunks of an Aleppo pine tree. This is Ehrlich's creation of courtyard. In the courtyard living room two Boomerang chairs are by Richard Neutra; leather poufs, Moroccan rugs and even the colours echo the souks of the architect's travels.

absorbing it to let out slowly when the air is cooler. Because temperature in hot, dry climates tends to fall considerably after sunset, the result is a thermal flywheel effect – the building interior is cooler than the exterior during the day and warmer than it at night. Buildings subject to diurnal fluctuations have traditionally been built with thick walls from materials with high mass such as adobe or masonry. Furthermore, windows are generally limited on most faces, with larger openings carefully positioned to avoid full-strength summer sun (which may anyway be too high in the sky to shine in) but perhaps admit some sunshine in winter when its warmth is more welcome.

In a hot, humid climate, however, building is quite different, since night temperatures do not drop considerably below daytime highs: with no need for insulation, lighter materials with little thermal capacity, but perhaps more scope for ventilation or resistance to rot, may be preferred. In some hot, moist climates, nonetheless, materials such as masonry are common, as they function as a desiccant. Roofs and walls may be protected from the sun's heat by overhangs or plant materials, which grow readily in the humidity. Here large wall openings should be positioned primarily on opposing sides of the envelope to catch breezes and encourage through ventilation.

wood

In our minds, wooden houses may belong equally in cold climates and warm – indeed anywhere there is enough moisture for trees to grow – but we tend to envisage cute log cabins or airy beach huts rather than architect-designed houses. In other words, we think of small properties when considering a wooden home, the poorer neighbour or first-time country home, for example, but this preconception should really by now be outmoded: wood is perfectly acceptable for larger, more permanent homes and certainly shouldn't be sniffed at as a contemporary building material. On the contrary, it is beautiful and good for us in several ways.

Many of the world's great buildings are made from wood, yet wood is often undervalued or ignored in the history of architecture. It is a material with unique qualities of form, colour and structure. From the sweeping eaves of Todaiji temple in Japan (the world's largest wooden building, dating from 1709), or the Baroque blockwork of Kizhi Island's cathedral in Russia (1714) with its powerful onion domes, to the willowy iroko-wood

construction by Renzo Piano for the Cultural Centre in Noumea, New Caledonia, of 1998 (which has to be one of the most modern structures on the planet), wood has shown versatility and ability to evolve in all ways, including stylistically. I was delighted to see glass-and-steel maniac Sir Norman Foster design a superlative structure of wood in Switzerland's Engadine valley a couple of years ago; sourcing material locally minimised transportation costs as well as fuel consumption. Foster is proud of these environmental credentials and I think other architects should follow suit.

Those building with wood are using the world's most renewable and environmentally friendly building product. In its 1976 report, CORRIM, the Consortium for Research on Renewable Industrial Materials, endorsed wood's energy-efficiency. In recent years, environmental concerns have joined with energy-efficiency questions, and in 1998 CORRIM examined construction and performance of houses in the cold of Minneapolis and the humid heat of Atlanta, and found use of wood in both locations presented

LEFT Solid wood flooring, and furniture offer potential generations of hard use. Their beauty is not skin-deep. They can live with nicks and scratches and are easily repaired and refinished. Coatings and finishes add to durability.

THIS PAGE This house on the Tasman Sea was painstakingly built with a team of three carpenters. Wood is a natural material that changes appearance with time and seeks balance with its surroundings.

BELOW Wood, particularly the blond or bleached variety, has become a very modern look for use in the domestic environment although timber is a material that has scarcely seemed at the forefront of technology in recent times.

RIGHT Plywood is used liberally in this house in France, resulting in a simple vocabulary and homogenous build. It takes confidence to apply ply to interiors since its appearance is not always the obvious or classic choice. Here it is splendid in its vastness.

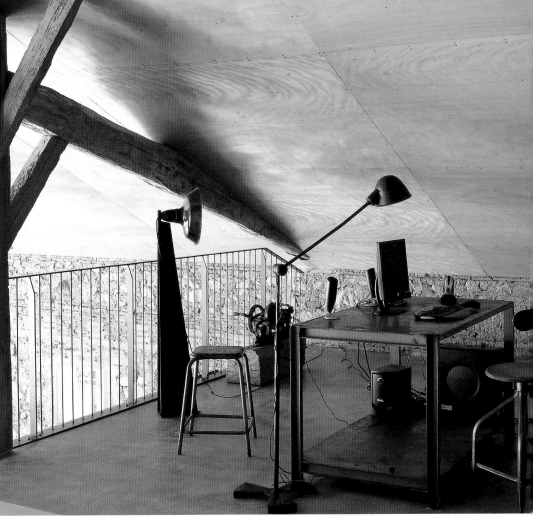

LEFT In a new build in France, beams and other structural elements are reclaimed wood, as are stair risers. The Mobile Light, which moves gently in air currents and further serves to accent the wood feature by night, is by Paul Verburg.

ABOVE A major feature of the living area in this California home has been formed by the addition of beautiful walnut *tansu*-style stairs. *Tansu* are traditional Japanese cabinets or chests, hence the stairs here also serve as storage.

ABOVE With flooring, moisture passes mainly through the end grain, so cut or mitred ends should be sealed with a transparent sealer before installation. Expansion and contraction of wood is normal during changes in the weather.

ABOVE RIGHT In a new but traditional extension to a waterside home at Goose Creek on Long Island, a very American nautical feel has been created by using painted wooden boards for walls throughout. Even these will change as they age.

significantly less environmental risks than steel- or concrete-frame options. The results demonstrated wood's benefits in almost all of five categories: embodied energy, global-warming potential, air-emission index, water emissions and solid waste. Further research found using steel frames alone to generate 33 percent more greenhouse-gas emission than wooden ones, and concrete a staggering 80 percent more. Using wood products reduces the need to burn fossil fuels to make or transport concrete or steel. Forests can be regenerated and, while much of the carbon from a harvested forest remains in wood products, new trees remove more carbon from the air.

Aside from general environmental benefits, wood is unsuited to desert regions, where trees are scarce and wood shrinks as it dries out. In humid climates, however, although the wrong wood will rot easily, local wood can be ideal. But use of tropical hardwoods requires caution, since their felling may deplete rainforest resources that take centuries to recover.

In any hot zone, particularly a humid one, wood is at risk from insects such as termites. Prevention is better than cure – usually toxic chemicals. Treating or sealing gives some protection, but best is to avoid direct contact with the ground, through concrete, steel or masonry foundations.

THIS PAGE Architects increasingly reveal wood in all its beauty. Exposed ceiling joists and joinery throughout a house in Auckland (top centre) place visual emphasis on the spaces as opposed to the ornament. Some alternatives to solid wood (top right) are wood veneers – thin slices of wood bonded to composite boards or plywood. This type of construction is often described as "all wood". What looks like solid hardwood may be something else: it pays to ask questions and take a hard look at materials.

ABOVE Hardwoods are deciduous trees with broad leaves, generally dormant in winter. Temperate varieties include oak, ash, cherry, maple and poplar, while mahogany, rosewood, teak and wenge are among the invaluable hardwoods from tropical forests. Aside from aesthetic considerations, substitutes can't compare with hardwoods when it comes to holding nails and screws and withstanding stresses and abrasions of daily life. Hardwoods for use in the home are carefully kiln-dried for that purpose, and will take on or give off moisture with extreme changes in humidity. When the air is exceptionally warm and humid, solid hardwoods absorb moisture and expand. With cooler, drier air, they give off moisture and contract. Softwoods or conifers have needles and are quick to regrow. Widely available species include cedar, fir, hemlock, pine, redwood, spruce and cypress. In a home, softwoods are used mainly as structural lumber such as 2x4s and 2x6s, with some limited decorative applications.

stone

IN A HOT, DRY CLIMATE, NOTHING CAN BEAT THE COOL, INSULATING SOLIDITY AND DURABILITY OF A THICK STONE WALL, THE LOCAL ROCK BLENDING WITH ITS NATURAL SURROUNDINGS.

Natural stone offers weight, opacity and a variety of patination. Not only does it look at home in its local environment, but it is suited to the climatic conditions, and hence extremely durable; and in hot, dry surroundings demanding materials with high thermal mass for insulation, it fits the bill beautifully. For these reasons, and to avoid transport costs, stone should be quarried as close to a site as possible – although small amounts of decorative rock may be transported from elsewhere.

Building with stone can nonetheless be costly and time-consuming. Just as organising and erecting a stone castle in past centuries was a daunting task involving enormous outlays of material, manpower, time and money, so today. But, like their forebears, new stone houses will live on and display status and substance. While stone somehow contradicted the popular image of early modernism, now contemporary architects are looking to its ancient values to give new expression to their ideas.

ABOVE View House in Knysna, South Africa, is a bastion-type sandstone structure. The sandstone within the main courtyard here has been cut into regular forms and the wall executed more like brickwork. The effect is still rough-hewn.

ABOVE RIGHT A cast-concrete bath from Get Real Surfaces and Charlemagne mosaic floor from US firm Waterworks give texture to an Arizona bathroom. Limestone walls, cool to touch, accentuate other finishes and textures.

Stonemasonry originated with dry-stacked stonework, where walls are carefully layered up without mortar, gravity serving as the binder that holds everything together. Freestanding dry-stacked stone walls are usually larger at the base and taper in slowly as the height increases. For absolutely no expense but labour costs, Irish farmers would build miles upon miles of stone walls this way, and low dry-stacked stone walls are ideal for landscaping projects.

Where "mortar" was first used, it was often merely mud or limestone plaster with little strength, which functioned as caulking to stop the flow of air rather than cementing stones together. Traditional mortared stone walls evolved with the emergence of cement mortar, made of burnt gypsum or lime mixed with water to make a paste with slight bonding capability. Stone walls still had to be built carefully: the paste just filled the gaps between stones and cured to form a soft, rock-like substance.

THIS PAGE Floating House in Kyalami, South Africa, by Slee & Co is a house for entertaining, almost an elliptical barge with all spaces flowing into one another and opening up directly to the water's edge. To the north is a moat-like swimming pool; here, to the south, the kitchen floats on a *koi* carp pond with a curved local-stone wall as backdrop.

The formula for modern cement originated in England in 1824. Called "Portland cement" because its colour is similar to rock from the Portland peninsula, it is made with limestone or chalk calcium, plus alumina and silica from clay and shale. The ingredients are ground, burnt in a kiln at about 1,350°C (2,500°F), fused into chunks, cooled and powdered. Gypsum is added to control setting speed, sand and water mixed in for a smooth mortar, often with lime for flexibility. With Portland cement it is possible to build a tall stone wall that does not taper inward. But although stones are "glued" together, stoneworking techniques are still important. Building a stone wall is an art, requiring time and skill.

Veneered stone walls are easier to build, and most stonework today (exceptions include the houses in this book by Johann Slee and Andrzej Zarzycki) consists of a non-structural veneer of stone against a structural wall of concrete (see pages 136–9) or breeze block. The structural wall is erected first, then

ABOVE LEFT Slate covers floors inside and out (on decks) at this Napa, California, house. Hardwearing floor materials include sandstone, York stone, granite and limestone. Slate, a dense non-porous stone that varies in colour, is extremely popular but usually off-limits because of its relative cost.

ABOVE CENTRE In keeping with local-authority requirements, a new build in Provence uses blocks of local limestone to create the appearance of an age-old structure.

ABOVE Entry to the Knysna courtyard, South Africa. Sandstone is a sedimentary rock composed of small grains cemented together by siliceous, felspathic or calcareous material. Its colour varies, depending on the binding material, from red through brown,

greenish, yellow, grey and white. Durability also depends on the cementing material, while porosity varies from low to very low.

LEFT Robert Dallas's wide, low South of France houses use traditional local stone and components with total authenticity, maintaining continuity with old Provençal style whilst adapting to modern ways of life.

RIGHT Limestone is a sedimentary rock formed at the bottom of lakes and seas with the accumulation of calcium-rich shells and bones. Calcareous stones readily dissolve in acid, so acidic products should never be used on them. Limestone that will take a polish is considered marble by most people, but if shells are visible or it is not crystalline, it is technically limestone.

LEFT In a former Italian monastery, now a home, marble dust was added to resin for the flooring, providing substance and deep texture. Pure resin, while easy to clean, might appear too plastic. The quartz aggregate means varying texture and skid-resistance.

BELOW LEFT Stone is the preferred hard surface for bathrooms, hard-wearing and easy to clean (whereas porcelain chips). It can be cut with a geometric hard edge or left *au naturel* – here a combination. Marble, limestone and travertine are popular but costly.

BELOW CENTRE Mosaics occur worldwide, often in local patterns. Here in Marrakech an outdoor water feature has a black stone mosaic splashback. Mosaic can be hand cut and applied piece by piece, or supplied in pre-planned patterns with numbered elements.

BELOW RIGHT A hard-wearing and economic product is mosaic sold in ready-made patterns mounted on paper to make it easy to lay, or terrazzo marble chips, plain or multi-coloured, set in cement and then ground to a smooth finish or left rocky.

BOTTOM The shower in the main bathroom of Johann Slee's Johannesburg house. Although much of the house is open to the elements, this is an indoor shower made to look alfresco by its dry-packed sandstone wall: a very interesting feature.

thin, flat stones are glued to its face with cement mortar. Metal tabs in the wall are mortared between stones to tie it all together and avoid the stonework peeling off. The structural wall serves as a form to make it really simple to lay the stones, provided they have good flat edges to work with.

A slipformed wall might be described as a cross between a traditional mortared stone wall and a veneered one. It is the method of stonemasonry many building firms use the most. Short forms, up to 0.6m (2ft) feet tall, are placed on both sides of a wall as a guide for stonework. Stones are then placed inside the forms, with their good profiles against the form. Then concrete is poured in behind the rocks, and reinforcing steel bar may be added for strength. This kind of wall can be faced with stone on one or both sides. With slipforms it is easy even for a novice to build a freestanding stone wall.

On one hand, stone retains a power to speak of ancient tradition; on the other, it is emblematic of the precise techniques utilised in modern structures. Many contemporary architects have explored stone architecture for civic buildings. For instance Rafael Moneo's city hall in Murcia, Spain, was completed in 1999, while Richard Meier's Getty Center, Los Angeles, reinterprets stone as cladding, and Ortner and Ortner's Museum for Modern Art in Vienna (2001) uses stone differently again, as an extreme interpretation of the most contemporary museum – the rectilinear form and colour of the anthracite standing out against Vienna's less radical museum quarter.

The 20th century saw a shift in relationship between architecture and stonemasonry, as architects became disengaged from the ancient craft of creating. Our culture must now redress this: architects should be willing to work alongside stone specialists and explore once more the nature of "stacking", which is an intrinsic part of building with stone since it involves the spaces between the stone. Then we may begin to see more buildings where "stoniness" is a feature, not merely a building material.

earth & brick

FAR MORE PREVALENT THAN STONE WALLS IN PARTS OF THE WORLD SUCH AS AFRICA, CHINA, SOUTHEAST ASIA AND MUCH OF INDIA IS MUD, IN ALL ITS TACTILE, COOLING GLORY.

The insulation qualities of mud are supreme – it is packed with air – and it is just lovely to the touch of the hand. Transportation costs are almost nil and, while generally not as durable as stone, earthen structures do last. The US government recently documented over 350,000 currently extant earthen houses and structures in the USA: many have survived with minimal maintenance for the past hundred years, and some were built as long ago as the 1600s.

Earthen buildings encompass a wide range, from those of simple rammed earth (which has low tensile strength and must usually be reinforced), through earth plaster over other cores, to the use of earthen bricks of many kinds (baked by the sun or in a kiln), including rustic adobe and clay-based brick. Soils themselves come in many guises, as any potter or gardener will tell you, some much more alkaline than others. It is this variability that makes multi-storeyed earthen buildings possible in the High Atlas of North

Africa or in northern Yemen, for example, but not in other regions. Soils formed under coniferous forests are extremely acidic and unsuitable for building, whereas those in deciduous forest or grassland can be widely used for construction, as in Western Europe and North America.

Desert soils, with their relatively high sand content, make an effective building material, while the arid heat greatly assists drying of bricks. Such earth bricks are common in the Middle East, North Africa, parts of Europe (notably Spain) and parts of the Americas. The Arabs brought their technique of *atobe* – making sun-dried bricks – to Spain, where it became adobe, as it is known through Hispanic America and increasingly worldwide. Adobe is essentially building with mud and straw, and can go horribly wrong unless the rules, derived from centuries of experience, are adhered to.

Blocks of adobe may be hand-moulded, but using moulds produces sharper edges and standard dimensions, facilitating bonding. Bricks are

OPPOSITE All openings in rammed-earth walls must have lintels to span the opening and support the earth above. Thick walls may need special detailing to accommodate manufactured windows.

ABOVE FAR LEFT Brick, made from clay and sand, is highly recyclable. Reclaimed brick, available through salvage companies, is often desired for its weathered appearance. Damaged brick can be crushed and recycled, to make more brick or for landscaping.

ABOVE LEFT & ABOVE Walls of hollow concrete blocks in brick-like

configuration work well in areas of seismic activity like New Zealand (above) and California (above left). Steel rods are inserted into the hollow blocks and wet concrete poured around them. Once hardened, it has great strength.

FAR LEFT & LEFT Waterproof finishes for soil-based materials such as cement stucco are more permanent but expensive, and trap moisture, which may be problematic. Permeable finishes such as mud plaster are less durable but inexpensive, and allow walls to absorb and give off airborne moisture.

moulded in a simple wooded frame, usually thin and square, then knocked out and stacked on end to dry. In building, the bricks are bonded by a wet mud of the same consistency, so bricks and mud dry and weather at the same rate. These bricks behave quite like stone when they dry out, and if not well compacted they shear and crack easily. Consequently, adobe is mainly used for load-bearing walls in compression, but it is not unusual to see it employed in other ways – including timberless domes which utilise the corbelling technique (in Syria, for example), where the building forms are egg-like in section, efficiently distributing the stresses.

Adobe is often finished with a plaster of mud and straw to give a smooth, rendered surface, reducing wind erosion. Some countries, such as Iran, favour dung as an emulsifying covering: this combination mud plaster is called *kar-gel*. With time, each region has developed its own method of constructing with mud. To bind well for building, soils must contain larger pieces of coarse sand as well as small sand particles, silt and fine clay. Clay is mixed with water and straw or similar material and mashed to the right consistency. Hybrid adobe is a revolutionary building material used to create low-cost insulated homes and other structures. It combines recycled paper with earth, sand and a binder to create a sustainable, inexpensive, strong, fibred material that can be poured, sprayed or sculpted.

While on the subject of earth, I think it important to mention "earth coupling": the percentage of a building's skin in contact with the earth. From season to season, even in a relatively constant warm climate, air temperatures can fluctuate greatly. Unlike air, earth maintains practically constant temperatures year-round, and the deeper you dig into the earth, the more constant and moderate the temperature. Thus insulation efficiency increases with the depth of the earth connection, and excavated earth is often then piled up against exterior walls to deflect winds, reduce air infiltration and increase the depth of earth coupling.

Recently mud has become fashionable in urban settings. Architect Glenn Murcutt, for example, in Sydney began to build massive walls of rammed earth and raw concrete in the late 1980s, moving away from steel-and-glass shoeboxes. Mud is seeing a resurgence as a building material worldwide, with the masters leading the way, and it is a truly delightful one.

glass

GLASS IS CRISP AND GIVES GORGEOUS REFLECTIONS, PARTICULARLY IN CITYSCAPES. DESPITE HEATING UP, IT CAN BE USED TO REGULATE INDOOR TEMPERATURE AS WELL AS PROVIDING A WINDOW ON THE WORLD OUTSIDE.

It might seem that people who live in glass houses should not live in warm climates, since large areas of glass trap the sun's heat, making it difficult to maintain ambient temperature (and we do not want to rely on air conditioning, do we?). That steamy, greenhouse-like effect is even greater in humid regions. Yet windows can mean ventilation, valuable in both dry and humid heat, and a dark, glassless building is just not appealing, not to mention wasting the sun's energy. The trick is to find a balance and to use glass cleverly as well-positioned windows for optimum views while encouraging it to work in your house's (and bank balance's) favour.

Glass has advantages in a warm climate, since it can help to reduce energy costs by drawing in the sun, carefully, to maintain a stable interior temperature. There are various ways of doing this, be it

LEFT Brick, wood or concrete walls are characterised by surface, glass by depth. Glass walls define space but do not enclose it, going against the grain of interior versus exterior. This house is 90% glazed.

ABOVE Used cleverly, glass can even out heat. A building benefits from "direct gain" when solar rays pass through a window and warm a surface in a living space. The more exposed to the sun, the greater the gain.

TOP RIGHT In Arizona, 5.8m (19ft) of floor-to-ceiling glass reveals the wilderness. Today we can have glass that is climate sensitive, or that allows insiders to see out but is opaque to passers-by – not an issue here.

ABOVE RIGHT In Steven Ehrlich's California home, a glass-and-steel tension bridge spans the living area. The house maximises volume and light, the glass bridge adding transparency to an open-plan room.

through solar panels (which can be mightily expensive) or the "passive" methods considered here. Essentially, passively heated and cooled buildings rely on sun, wind and surrounding earth to maintain comfortable interior temperatures. Hence orientation plays an enormous part in window design.

For the best passive solar performance, the area of sun-facing glazing should be 7 to 12 percent of a building's floor area; many successful Californian houses, for instance, have approximately 12 percent window area to the south (since this is the northern hemisphere) and 2–3 percent on east, west and north sides. Overhangs can be key, providing shade for sun-facing windows in summer yet allowing low-angled sun to penetrate in winter when more heat is needed; they are not so useful for east- or west-facing windows since sun from the east or west is low in the sky (nor nearer the tropics, where summer sun is overhead). Of course we do not all seek passive solar gain: some homes have their main windows positioned precisely to avoid direct sun, while others give priority to views, but hot homes rarely invite heat in indiscriminately with large windows on all sides.

A more complex way of warming interiors is the thermal-storage wall, typically a dark masonry wall positioned between exterior glazing and living space. It absorbs the sun's rays by day and radiates heat in the evening when it is cooler. Thermal-storage walls occupy little space and are particularly effective in winter, when low sun angles strike them most directly. Another energy-saving device is "sun spaces", glass rooms built onto the sunny side of a building to collect heat, like a conservatory. These rooms are thermally isolated from the rest of the building so their interiors heat quickly. The hot air is released directly into the building via windows, doors or vents. Such spaces can, for example, speed early-morning warm-up in a climate where nights are cool, such as a desert environment.

Solar windows increase the insulating properties of glass. These are double-glazed windows with twice the R-value (the measurement of thermal resistance) of single-glazed. A new type with a thin film between the glass layers that reflects long-wave radiation has an R-value over four times that of single glazing. If the space between the glass is filled with argon gas the R-value can double again.

Speciality window coatings can boost the energy efficiency of windows. The "low-E2" variety is good for hot climates because, in addition to improving the insulating ability of windows, it limits solar heat gain by blocking infrared and some ultraviolet rays. In some cases, solar-control glass can reduce cooling loads so much that cooling-system capacity can be cut or glass area added without increasing the loads. It offers the greatest energy savings where cooling costs are higher than heating costs.

ABOVE Oh, the luxury of a picture window in one's bathroom. There are numerous courtyards in this Marrakech home and much of the house is in relative shade. The window makes the most of courtyard privacy.

ABOVE This New Zealand house has a glazed screen with an expressed colonnade stretching between block walls. Wooden shields, with strips of glass louvre, give shelter from summer sun (and neighbours).

RIGHT Just as a structural overhang can keep out summer sun but allow in low-angled winter rays, so in Johann Slee's South African house, trees provide natural shelter. The picture window draws the outside in.

concrete

A PLIABLE AND POETIC MATERIAL, IN MANY CASES, PARTICULARLY WHEN USED WITH OTHER MATERIALS, CONCRETE HAS A SURPRISING LIGHTNESS OF TOUCH. ALTHOUGH THERE ARE ENVIRONMENTAL ISSUES, IT HAS POTENTIAL FOR HOT-CLIMATE BUILDING.

LEFT In the underbelly of the house built by Helena Arahuete in Napa, California, concrete plays a major role – only the floor is slate. Concrete walls mimic the knotted wood that supported them in construction.

ABOVE Pigment can be added to concrete for colour – it does not have to be the usual grey. Here the floor is anthracite-coloured concrete.

ABOVE RIGHT Some people prefer a rough-hewn look and choose to leave a poured floor

pitted and mottled on the surface. Concrete is frequently used alongside earth in builds since its stability affords earth greater strength and the two sit well together.

ABOVE FAR RIGHT Others like to contrast different concrete finishes – polished concrete is popular as it is easy to sweep and wash. It can give a clinical edge to a room or just a more polished one in every sense. Concrete floors are extremely durable if correctly made.

Among the worries and concerns for global warming, we have a serious problem with concrete. Although it behaves beautifully in a warm climate – it is good for insulation, absorbing and storing warmth, and highly durable (plus resistant to insects), even in heat or humidity – and is relatively inexpensive and quicker to build with than stone or other laborious methods, its production certainly does not help the environment. Concrete is used pretty indiscriminately for public and private builds and contributes an estimated massive 10–12 percent of carbon dioxide emissions in the world, due to a combination of sheer volume produced and the very high temperatures required to create the core Portland cement (see page 124) used in the standard process.

Concrete consists of Portland cement mixed with sand, gravel and water. The larger particles of gravel interlock like little fingers to make the concrete resistant to cracking. Steel reinforcing bar can be added to serve as much longer fingers. Vast amounts of energy are required for the blast furnaces making cement, and this comes most often from burning coal. Attempts at energy-efficiency and CO_2 reduction in the cement industry have been, up to now, concentrated on small improvements in furnace technology and replacing coal with waste oil and other refuse where possible (and profitable).

Great amounts of CO_2 are also released as concrete dries. This de-gassing is a result of the key reaction in hardening, so it has been widely assumed that there is no possibility for improvements. But at Luleå University in Sweden, a Russian guest researcher has spearheaded a new grinding process for cement and sand which cracks the grains so that they add more effectively to the strength of the concrete, and the quantity of cement can be reduced by half without compromising strength. This new technology reduces emissions radically, both in production and during curing. Since it is also profitable, there is a good chance of decreasing the world's CO_2 emission by about 3 percent just by its use.

Alternatives to traditional concrete include some which take less energy to make, have better thermal properties, or make use of materials which otherwise would have become landfill. But each has its drawbacks, typically in cost – one reason why concrete remains so popular is economy. Recently, however, CSIRO, the Australian science and industrial research office, announced the development of a form of concrete called HySSIL. According to Dr Swee Liang Mak, who leads the CSIRO team, "'HySSIL is a revolutionary aerated cementitious [cement-based] product that is as strong as normal concrete but is only half as heavy. It provides up to five times the thermal insulation of concrete and is also impact and fire resistant. HySSIL wall panels are also expected to offer significant cost advantages over existing products." HySSIL is easier to recycle than traditional concrete, more resistant to earthquakes (because of lower density and lighter weight), and is made of non-toxic material. The lower cost comes from a combination of lower energy use for manufacturing and lower transport expenses because of its light weight; the latter also greatly reduces the cost of use.

In a warm climate, building with any type of concrete has pitfalls and needs tight control. Hot-weather problems include quicker drying and evaporation, so more water is used, reducing potential strength; it may mean less air within the concrete, hence less insulation; and fast setting times may be inconvenient. But on the whole concrete is durable, adaptable and has high thermal mass – particularly advantageous in a climate that is warm by day and cooler at night.

A year or two ago I would have thought twice about advocating use of concrete (since I have three children, I am mightily concerned for the environment). But with some concretes now developed that actively absorb CO_2, I am having a change of heart. Although it will take a lot to educate the industry to be as environmentally aware as it should be, concrete need no longer be the bad apple of building.

BELOW FAR LEFT High temperature, wind and humidity can all have a negative impact on concrete's performance, although higher humidity tends to reduce the effects of heat. Concrete is used here in a three-storey essentially earth house.

BELOW LEFT Concrete may crack due to a rapid drop in temperature, for instance if a slab or wall is placed on a very hot day, followed by a cool night typical of desert. Trust the experts if you require a flawless floor.

BELOW During building, heat makes water evaporate from concrete surfaces more quickly and the concrete stiffens earlier, increasing the chances of plastic cracking. Scoring helps prevent mass cracks.

RIGHT For successful placement of concrete in hot climates, be sure you have enough workers to avoid delays placing, finishing and curing, and consider early-morning or evening placement. That said, stairs are relatively easily constructed in concrete.

metal

WE TEND TO ASSUME THAT METAL HEATS
UP TOO READILY FOR USE IN A HOT
CLIMATE – THE CLASSIC HOT TIN ROOF –
BUT WITH THE RIGHT FINISH IT WILL
REFLECT THE SUN AND HELP PREVENT A
HOUSE OVERHEATING. IT IS ALSO LIGHT,
CHEAP AND DURABLE.

It was not until selecting projects for this book that I began to understand the advantages of using metal in a hot climate; I was frankly surprised to see it so readily applied, for example as roofing in the dry Arizona heat or for window frames in dusty Marrakech. Metal has a low thermal mass, so does not store heat by day and release it at night. But with the right structure and finish (such as white paint) it will deflect the sun's rays, and can also be made to transfer heat to water supplies.

Metal's predominant – although not only – use in hot-climate builds is for roofing. Metal roofing has a very long history, with roofs in the United

OPPOSITE Whether used for window frames, roofing or anywhere around the house, paint finishes on metal shed dirt and do not support the growth of algae or fungal matter, which is particularly important if the climate is humid. Paints used on "cool" metal roofing also resist chalking and colour fade.

ABOVE LEFT, TOP In Provence, a unique and artful security door is hand-forged iron. Because of metal's malleability, it can provide a decorative option even when fulfilling a primary function. The grille-like effects formed by metal, whether forged, woven or laser-cut, add an element of airiness to a warm house.

ABOVE LEFT, BOTTOM There are definite advantages to selecting metal over wood for door and window frames: a wooden window frame weathers with age, and expands and contracts according to weather conditions. It also requires three times more material than a metal frame, reducing the glazed area.

ABOVE The long life and low maintenance of metal roofing, combined with savings from energy efficiency, give it a very attractive life-cycle cost. Whereas unfinished (i.e. natural silvery-coloured) metal absorbs heat too readily, many finishes reflect and radiate it well.

States that date back to the 1800s still in service. Its durability (metal roofing products being manufactured today carry manufacturers' warranties lasting from 20 to 50 years) makes them a very low per-annum-cost option, and most new products are designed so that they can be refurbished on site for additional life. Painted metal roofs retain 95 percent of their initial reflectance and emittance over time.

Another plus is that metal (at 18–61kg per 9.3sq m/40–135lb per 100sq ft) is the lightest-weight roofing available for a serious build. This has a twofold benefit: it places less demand on a building's structure and is advantageous in locations prone to seismic activity – as indeed many hot regions are. In addition, the interlocking or active fastening of most modern metal roofing panels means that severe winds can pass through them without causing any damage.

Many metal roofs are formed in ways that stop heat transfer through conduction, by allowing only minimal contact between the metal and the underlying structure. "Cool" roofs, in various finishes, combine high solar reflectance and infrared emittance to keep the roof cool while protecting against sun damage and extending roof life.

LEFT Metal door frames require much less maintenance than wood. Metal is a durable material, and metal products are not subject to the degradation experienced by organic materials when exposed to moisture. Metal has a long life thanks to its ability to resist the elements, and a low maintenance cost.

ABOVE Aesthetically speaking, metal has extensive design flexibility and can be worked to suit many different styles of building due to its ability to accept coatings of various colours and patterns. These wooden interior doors are covered in metal sheeting for subtle decorative effect.

ABOVE RIGHT, TOP On an environmental note, of which there are many in this chapter, metals are 100% recyclable if they are ever removed. Additionally, many metals used in new builds will have recycled content varying from 25% to 95%. Metal structure is light-weight and easy to install.

ABOVE RIGHT, BOTTOM Metal's building benefits are far greater than most people think in a hot climate. Just as we now appreciate its use in kitchens, where it is wipe-clean, and bug-free if cleaned regularly, so we are coming to see that it can be invaluable elsewhere in a hot home.

colour

in blue, for example, in dimly lit chapels because blue retains much of its intensity even in penumbra, so she shines above all else). In times past, ultramarine pigment used to be rare, as it was produced by grinding down semi-precious lapis lazuli; today one source for indigo blue is woad, although perhaps surprisingly the E-coli bacterium can also produce it.

Colour is the first thing you notice about a room, so if you are keen to go bold, make sure you are really convinced before committing yourself to a decorative scheme. No one says, "Did you see that room with the picture window and metal beams?" No, they say, "Did you see the green room?" So please ensure it is a green room you wish to be remembered for; in my opinion the most successful hot houses beg the phrase, "Did you see the view?" – the mark of a true genius build.

LEFT In Karim El Achak's Moroccan guesthouse, red plays a starring role. Iron-oxide pigments have constituted the basic palette of artisans from Egypt to India and China since history began, with associations of blood or good luck.

BELOW FAR LEFT Flat painted grey is often unwelcoming but charcoal mottled-textured walls can be quite special – like the best flannel suit. Used dramatically in its darkest guise, grey is a good mental shelter.

BELOW LEFT Just as cool colours encourage rest and meditation, hot colours promote activity. However, too much of the red spectrum can be distracting and draining, so use it carefully, particularly in hot climes.

BELOW Muriel Brandolini's US Hampton Bays home is awash with colour: no surprise, since the French-Vietnamese-Venezuelan designer is renowned for her colour sense. She admits to using an "ocean of bright paint" throughout her waterfront house.

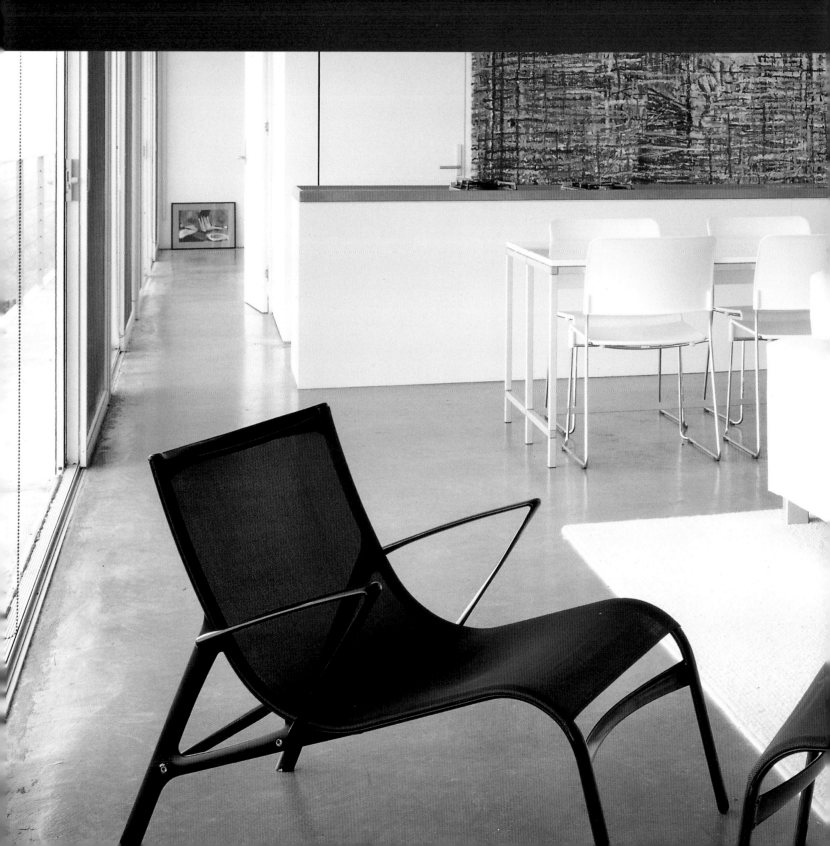

furnishing

Some of the most diverse and dynamic regions of the world boast hot homes set in bucolic landscapes. Distinct architectural traditions have evolved from geographical, cultural and historical circumstances, including imports – architectural and furnishings – from Holland, Spain and England, of sometimes dubious appropriateness to their new climate (some elements just do not travel well). It is best, in many cases, to leave them at home and start afresh with new eyes. Contemporary modern houses in these disparate lands have common threads in that they tend to share an openness and sympathetic spirit with the tenets of modernism while remaining true to the particulars of place. The modernist house is fluid, informal, spacious, with porous boundaries between indoor and out; it is a good blueprint for interior form to follow.

Italian architect and furniture designer Antonio Citterio has much to say about building in the more remote parts of the world. Australians, he says, "focus on the real qualities and values in their life – family, relationships, food, the natural. I like these people who do not seem under stress," he adds, "unlike, for example, New Yorkers."

It is an easy-going attitude that shapes the way we live in a hotter climate, a more relaxed arena in general. We build homes for socialising, so we need a good sofa or two, a decent table to eat at, even if it is outside, good bathrooms, and perhaps an outdoor shower for that feeling of freedom, of being at one with nature. The great outdoors is usually the starting point for a hot home, and the design upshot is a deep-seated sensitivity to landscape. Use devices that bring outdoors in; blur the boundary.

Indigenous materials, we know, work well in tropical and subtropical climates, as they do everywhere, but further concern must be given to the rareness of some materials, including hardwoods. The increasing use of bamboo, for example, in interior design, is encouraging and hopeful: with its rapid growth and excellent durability, it is the logical replacement for many rare woods, and with the development of techniques that allow the manufacture of flat sheets of material from bamboo canes, the idea of bamboo design has taken on a more solid shape.

As with the shells of buildings, technology coupled with sensitivity to natural materials, including fabrics, should be the guiding force for interiors. Currently it is primarily people with artistic drive and ideas of their own who design furniture using materials such as bamboo. Soon, I am sure, *haute couture* and mass-market designers will catch up, and we will see even slicker interiors made from appropriate materials.

cooking & eating

FOOD AND SHELTER ARE
OUR MOST FUNDAMENTAL
NEEDS, AND THE HISTORY
OF FOOD CAN TELL THE
STORY OF TIME AND PLACE.

The communal nature of eating, once a norm for us all, seems to have endured better for some reason in warmer climates than in temperate lands. Perhaps it is that the heat makes us prone to pause a while in the shade and ingest slowly, rather than refuelling on the run while multi-tasking. Eating outdoors certainly adds to the pleasure.

It is quite incredible how centuries ago people wandered the planet sharing ideas, and changed foreign palettes by introducing spices, exotic fruits and customs – and how just the breaking of bread together can initiate peace. Istanbul was once the beating heart of the Ottoman Empire, a crossroads where civilisations and cultures from Europe, Asia and the Middle East met and traded. Discovering culinary delights played a significant role wherever the Ottomans travelled. They would carry with them their *kazan*, a large cooking pot in which all the ingredients collected on their journeys were

ABOVE A central work-station results in an airy kitchen with sightlines. Better to face guests or empty space than a wall. Good design is essential to a kitchen; the triangle philosophy (sink, fridge, cooker), from 1950s studies in ergonomics, works well.

RIGHT In Marrakech the KO team created a cave-like kitchen that is very functional, a blend of old

techniques and modern form. A modern *tadelak* equivalent, varnished concrete, gives a brutal but shimmering effect. Cupboard doors are uncut sardine-can sheets.

OPPOSITE Marble and stainless steel evoke cleanliness and cool. Again in Morocco, we find double square basins and workstation, and space for two or three people to work at once.

A little spit and polish was all it took to clean up this kitchen in the original part of a converted 1960s American house. Keeping a kitchen tidy must be effortless, and utensils should be kept to the bare minimum.

cooked over an open fire. The *kazan* offered a rich tapestry of tastes and pleasures, many influences and kitchen tips coming into play. The fusion of history and taste is an extremely palatable one.

Certain foods have had an amazing influence on history. Potatoes, for instance, indigenous to South America, were probably brought to Europe around 1570, but were widely resisted. Until 1780, they were excluded from prudent French tables, as they were thought to cause leprosy. Devout Scottish Presbyterians refused to eat them because they weren't mentioned in the Bible, while in colonial Massachusetts they were considered the spoor of witches. Ireland was the first country to fully adopt the potato, and suffered terribly in the potato famine of 1845, triggering a wave of emigration.

Despite all the to-ings and fro-ings of food throughout history, my mother tells me she saw her first banana in England only as a late teenager around 1950, and I remember clearly my own experience in Paris, aged 11, when I discovered, to my great chagrin, that Diet Coke had not yet reached French soil! Food habits generally move quite swiftly, however, and I am glad to say that the house owners who kindly allowed us to photograph their homes for this book all seem to experiment with local flavours and buy local produce, thus doing their bit for the environment by reducing transportation. Moreover, they all understood that in a warm climate, cleanliness is particularly close to godliness.

One of the most interesting aspects of photographing this book was the lunch break: although we rarely expected it, we were given lunch while working (this might have had something to do with the

OPPOSITE, BELOW In a new build in Provence, the entire kitchen is custom-designed and handmade: it leads from dining room to hallway and reception, in true French *enfilade* spirit, thus it has to be smart. Even the rubbish bin is wood-encased, Shaker-like, designed by Andrzej Zarzycki.

RIGHT Architect Audrey Matlock designed this award-winning external dining room for financier Martin Harding near Sag Harbor, Long Island. Note the look-through fire area with suspended pulley shutter and state-of-the-art barbecue. Chairs are from French firm Triconfort and the table by Matlock.

BELOW In southern France a former barn was sensitively converted to provide modern comfort without expensive mod cons. Bugs proliferate in hot climes, so clean kitchens are vital: experts recommend using good old-fashioned bleach since newer antibacterial products have unlooked-for side-effects.

BELOW RIGHT Martin Harding's house is ideal for entertaining. He even keeps a box of cashmere blankets for guests for cooler evenings – true luxury. The structure provides shelter from extreme weather.

houses frequently employing staff), thus we too sampled the most delicious tagines of lamb in Marrakech, the best cuts of beef, barbecued, in America, and the freshest local fish, grilled, in South Africa. Food became a very important part of our journey through hot lands and something we greatly looked forward to on arrival, just like the Ottomans of old.

A unifying element of our culinary adventure was the lack of casual eating (meaning no TV dinners). Lunch was a relaxing and durable event, usually accompanied by rosé or other wine, just a little, and masses of water. It was, on the whole, served alfresco at midday (no later, to be able to squeeze in the ubiquitous siesta – not us, of course, since we had work to do) under arbours or sun shades, often by the pool or on the waterfront, and kept simple.

An added benefit to eating outdoors, and often cooking outside too, is that kitchens and rooms for eating remain cleaner – bugs and bacteria thrive so in a warm arena, particularly a humid one – and terraces can simply be swept. Kitchens can be uncluttered and aesthetically pleasing, although they must use materials that are easy to keep clean. Wood, despite its porosity, is very clean, harbouring less germs than plastic. It is also the most exquisite material to touch. Hence wood is a good choice for worktops and chopping boards, particularly temperate hardwoods – oak, beech and maple – which are strong and easy to maintain. Avoid tropical hardwoods in kitchens: they can be toxic if splintered.

TOP LEFT A myriad of woods create an extremely sophisticated space. The chameleon-like kitchen blends into the altogether seamless house (this is my kind of kitchen – truly, deeply chic). Breakfast stools and bar offer a view too.

BOTTOM LEFT Fabric, fashion and interior designer Muriel Brandolini and husband Nuno bought their Hampton Bays waterfront spread a couple of years ago and made a jewel out of it, using her signature bright colours. The linear kitchen is open plan to the main living room.

ABOVE Mesh bar stools by Harry Bertoia nestle under a stone overhang in an essentially wood kitchen. When buying a new wood kitchen, look for environmentally responsible companies and wood from sustainable sources.

RIGHT, ABOVE Oh the luxury of space. I live in a London townhouse, my dining room doubling as office. Here is the dream of two dining tables, one formal, the other less so, just a few metres apart.

RIGHT Chairs in the right fabric provide comfort when dining inside. Since living in a hot climate often means a multitude of hard surfaces, fabric and upholstery are welcome, and help sound absorption.

FAR RIGHT In the South African beachside home, limed wood cabinetry, handle-less with good pop-out action, has been made specifically for the house. The lengthy table is for dining and acts as a boundary between the kitchen area and the rest of the voluminous ground floor.

FAR LEFT Hand-cut tiles are omnipresent in North Africa and the Middle East. Despite their strength and water-resistance, tiles are better for splashbacks than worktops, unless you use an epoxy grout or re-grout regularly, since grouting is easily stained. Vitrified tiles can work in any position.

LEFT Do not be fooled into thinking this is a bathroom. The tin basin is extremely deep and used for all manner of preparation in this African *rondavel* kitchen. Sinks should be shallow for comfort, but who can resist this beauty?

ABOVE & RIGHT To one end of a Provençal home, an almost medieval niche has been carved out of the house for relaxed evenings grilling. This is a true outdoor country kitchen, and even contains a rustic kind of worktop, where meat and veg are prepped. Logs are for use on the barbecue, which also adds warmth on cooler evenings. The only storage needed is for the timber, since plates and glasses are brought from the kitchen . Note the smart extractor hood.

OPPOSITE The colours of the outdoor chairs echo those inside, although the struts are in differing directions and the chair shape not the same – distant cousins. In a warm climate, the edges between indoor and out blur, and eating is often alfresco or at least at the cusp of the house boundaries. Here a link is made between the two via the furniture. A rustic setting can be effectively modernised with contemporary furniture and just a touch of accent colour.

living

NATURAL FABRICS AND GRASSES, PLUS AN UNDERSTANDING OF AIR CURRENT, HAVE TO BE THE KEY TO COMFORTABLE HOT LIVING, WHETHER INSIDE OR OUT.

Sitting room, living room, drawing room, lounge: what is it to be? The main "living" room of the house is given different names depending upon various factors that include physical location (country), the grandness of the house and occupiers' social background. It is true that we "lounge" in such a room but the noun does not, to me, seem appropriate as a generic term for the main "reception" room (to use the real-estate term) since it sounds too casual, too informal. Drawing room is simply too grand a description for the way most of us live (the term has its roots in the "withdrawing" capacity – from the days when the parlour existed) and sitting room implies not much else happens in the room but waiting – a kind of antechamber to living. So I will stick with living room since it conjures some kind of activity, even if it is just the lounging variety.

Living in a hot climate does mean adopting a slower pace at least some of the time, and time management has to come into play. Just as we water plants at dawn or dusk, we should too enjoy heightened activity at these periods of the day (an early swim or run, perhaps tennis) since by midday the sun will encourage little more than a hearty lunch and afternoon nap. Working in a hot climate is another matter, although time management remains the key to success; a home office should be in the coolest part of the house, or where the temperature is most constant (see Karim El Achak's subterranean room or Johann Slee's artist studio), and the working day should be split into two definite portions, spanning more hours on the whole but with a longer break in between.

The devices for keeping cool, whether at work or at play, remain the same, and great comfort can be achieved by the use of ceiling fans or understanding of air current. As a Londoner by birth and

LEFT In the main living quarter of a house built by Studio KO, windows are small so sunlight does not heat up the room by day. Furnishings, however, are warm, since evenings are cool in wintertime. The ottomans and rugs are local wares.

ABOVE This bookshelf in the east-facing study mimics the wrap form of the Melbourne house by BKK Architects. Although there is little place for clutter in a hot home, books are always welcome for stimulus and relaxation.

ABOVE With no central heating, fireplaces are integral to heating systems (unlike, ironically, in temperate climes, where they are often simply focal points). Karim El Achak's home delightfully blends Moroccan tradition and modernity.

currently by location, I am constantly amazed at how useless the Brits are at understanding convection and its relevance to traditional sash windows. These were invented so that you open the top by half and at the same time the bottom by half, so hot air escapes and cold air enters – so simple. Perhaps we have so few very warm days in the UK that the matter has not been dwelled upon – but in essence the instruction is clear: in any climate, get to know the physical capabilities of your architecture and use the spaces as they have been designed, since very little in architecture happens by accident. If you have louvres, play with them to achieve the coolest effect. Keep an eye on sun shades or scrim at windows and be aware of the damaging effect of the sun on furniture and fabrics (installing mechanical sun shades that rise and fall automatically has never, to my mind, been successful since on days with some clouds and intermittent sun the shades "go up and down like a whore's knickers", to quote photographer Ken Hayden).

Fabric plays an enormous role in keeping cool in a warm climate and again it is science that helps us. Sheep keep cool in summer and warm in winter, and true wool (the coat of the domestic sheep as opposed to the wool of goats – angora or cashmere) is a very good material for climates where seasons swing from one extreme to another, although it should be used wisely and does not adapt to every furniture possibility – cottons and linens are better coverings for chairs than wool in a warm climate. One of the reasons wool works well in both climatic extremes is its insulating quality, due to the pockets of air it holds in its natural state and retains when woven.

OPPOSITE, TOP A pair of vast, beautiful wooden hinged doors open in two swift moves in this Auckland home. Simple, well-defined furniture helps any home. Floor-to-ceiling louvred glass panels bring ventilation and some light.

OPPOITE, BOTTOM Mysterious dark walls are traditional for an African enclosure. Although rooted in history, many features, such as the built-in seating, appear contemporary. With little space, the only option is to run seating around the perimeter.

ABOVE Cabinets in African mahogany flank the door to a house by Collett-Zarzycki, hiding a bar and hi-fi. Neutral natural fabrics and animal hides give cool comfort (whereas leather can feel sticky); in low humidity, staining on fabrics is not an issue.

RIGHT In an art collector's home on Long Island, he and Annabel Selldorf curated a collection of mid-20th-century furniture befitting the house's 1960s origins. The graphic fabric of the settee brings an element of masculinity.

Silk can be used successfully too in a warm climate, but can be less durable and less equipped for moisture, so is wiser left alone or used for throws. The best fibres for comfort and durability are cotton, as a fabric and as wadding and padding, and linen. Cotton, incidentally, was first woven in pre-Inca Peru in around 200 BC, although the plant and fibre probably have origins in the Middle East since the word is derived from the Arabic *qutun*. Although now adapted to temperate growing zones, cotton, a species of spermatophyte (meaning seed-bearing), is a tropical plant and thrives best in high temperatures with a great deal of sunshine and abundant moisture. Like local woods that behave well in their own environments, cotton is durable and sturdy in moist, hot climates.

Linen is a luxury anywhere (it can be pricey) and particularly good in a hot climate – it remains cooler than the room temperature. It is good to wear, to lie in and to sit upon; enjoy the creases, do not try to fight them. Linseed-filled bags are useful cooling devices when placed on a forehead, in cases of over-heating or a post-luncheon hangover. Linen fabric has many advantages over cotton because of its structure. It has a less "woolly" surface and does not soil as readily nor, being less spongy, does it absorb and retain moisture as easily. It is grown in temperate and cool climates and in wintertime in the subtropics. A woody fibre obtained from the flax stem, linen is slightly heavier than cotton but has twice its strength. Visually, it sits well with slate, wood and stone, and is ideal for a rough-hewn, natural but elegant home.

LEFT Although a building merging with its landscape is a well-acknowledged idea for architects, when John Wardle created award-winning Balnarring Beach House, he decided not to draw the house into the landscape but to seek a balance by separating the two, "developing opportunities to extend and frame views". The house and garden, according to the architect, do not inhabit the same space.

ABOVE American Poet William Carlos Williams (1883–1963) penned, "Is it any better in Heaven, my friend Ford, Than you found it in Provence?" ("To Ford Madox Ford in Heaven"). There is something magical about Provençal light that conjures outdoor living. The perfect combination of azure-blue sky, home-grown materials and the scent of Provence – potent lavender and musty olive – just makes you want to sit outside!

RIGHT Just beyond the rear of the house built by Karim El Achak in the Moroccan city of Marrkech, a pergola shades alfresco life. Exterior living rooms have to be well shaded in the heat of the sun. Here, white calico covers reflect the sun and remain cool to touch. Clara Candido, El Achak's Italian wife, has an import-export business and many of the fabrics and objects are pieces she has collated.

bed

A GOOD BED IS FUNDAMENTAL TO LIFE ITSELF, AND SLEEP THE ONLY TRUE PANACEA TO PROBLEMS. UNADORNED BEDROOMS ARE SURELY THE MOST TRANQUIL, SO KEEP THEM SIMPLE AND PURE.

Sleeping alone in the heat is quite different from sleeping with someone, so ensure your bed is big enough to let you choose when to embrace and when to lie listless in solitude. Metaphysical poet John Donne had the right idea in "The Sun Rising": "This bed thy centre is, these walls thy sphere."

If the house works and the heat has been controlled by methods described earlier, the bedroom should be cool enough for slumber, although in some climates, particularly humid ones, even cooling does not mean total comfort. The best approach is to keep things simple and use empty space well: place the bed in the centre of the room so there is plenty of air circulating. Ensure it is raised from the ground with space underneath (box bed bases might be good for storage but increase heat and dust). Floors should be comfortable under bare feet, but rugs and carpets will often feel too hot or fusty.

ABOVE Floor-to-ceiling glazing gives light and a view. Blind mechanisms are hidden between ceiling and glazing, which cascades past floor level. The chair is re-edition Swan by Arne Jacobsen (designed 1957–8).

RIGHT A leather-upholstered inverted T frame supports a bed and, beyond the "wall", a sofa. This is the bedroom equivalent of a smart kitchen's central workstation, and works well in a warm climate.

RIGHT, ABOVE If you live in a region popular with guests, a bedroom chair can be a solace from the world. A good read and a view is all you need. In John Wardle's Balnarring house, sliding doors open gracefully to nature.

Pillows for head support should be kept to a minimum and fashion pillows should be avoided (no matter what the climate, there is rarely a place for a spare cushion).

Sheets should be cotton or linen and simple in plain whites or neutrals, and bedclothes should not sweep the floors as they will gather dust. Layering is key to comfortable sleeping, just as for clothing: different weights added one on top of another when temperatures drop. There is something reassuring about a little swaddling, and with cotton and linen you can lie wrapped and still keep cool. Linen is cool to the touch, and hence unparalleled in intense heat. Duvets are rarely needed in warm climates.

Many of the houses we visited incorporated large windows in bedrooms for the view. Witnessing the great outdoors from within can help reduce the feeling of claustrophobia in high temperatures. Better

still, if you can, attach a little outside space to the bedroom by way of a balcony or terrace, also lovely for early-morning breakfasts in peace (if you have guests then the fluster of hospitality can also make life more uncomfortable in a hot climate, so take it easy, pace yourself).

Some architects even switch the plan of a house to ensure the bedroom has features usually reserved for living spaces. Johann and Rene Slee's bedroom leads straight to the pool at the front of their South African house. Again in South Africa, Silvio Rech and Lesley Carstens leap from their bed into living since their bedroom, both logistically and emotionally, is the heartbeat of their home.

Storage is a necessity but the less movement the better in a warm house, so keep clothes folded neatly at waist height and hanging items easy to reach. A wardrobe, like a home, should always be edited to necessities — there is no place for surplus in the modern, contained world.

LEFT This South African room is very basic indeed, its built-in shelf and wall recess the only adornment. If it were not palatial it would appear almost cell-like! But is this not the way to live with all action outside?

ABOVE A bedroom requires just the basics, four walls and a bed, as long as there is room for storing clothes and good bathing facilities nearby, preferably *en suite*. This room, with its exposed brick, is rural French.

BELOW LEFT A child's room can be clutter-free, but should be a happy place. In Hampton Bays, New York, Muriel Brandolini has painted pretty horizontal stripes and created flora-inspired headboards.

BELOW As seen in this art dealer's home in the Hamptons, New York, I tend to prefer a high bed, the best crisp sheets, plump pillows and a jolly good mattress: a no-nonsense approach, almost hospital chic.

ABOVE Small spaces make sense in a second home, or where outdoors takes precedence. A rather neat structure houses all the necessary trappings for sleep and study away from home in this teenager's room.

RIGHT Decoration can be too visually stimulating, but smart, bold paint strokes add panache. In Marrakech, Karim El Achak and his wife's bedroom exhibits extreme tidiness yet robust character.

TOP, LEFT TO RIGHT The freestanding bath (here beside a low floating wall) is the original bathing system: the bath used to be a tub filled by hand. This is a modern version, unadorned and floating. Duravit makes very good systems.

A tailor-made sunken concrete bath for two, side-by-side, plus shower, in a scheme by Seth Stein. Sunken baths usually look good and may leave more space for a window. They are, however, quite difficult to negotiate, so beware.

This is a fantastic corridor of a bathroom where the bath simply fits between an exterior deck and the interior. Sliding panes offer protection if required. The enclosure has strong lines and a gorgeous blend of materials.

I prefer bathrooms that echo Greece and Rome. Here the proportions and mosaic tiles give a nod to the ancients, while modernity brings good lighting and an unlimited supply of water. The ladder is cleverly placed for towels.

BOTTOM, LEFT TO RIGHT Even a tiny bathroom can sport an ample period bathtub. Visual comfort is more important than physical comfort in a bathroom, as long as the bath is right. This mellow mix of warm woods is modern African serenity.

Mosaics are a traditional addition to a bathroom and these days usually appear in one colour for simplicity. Italian firm Bisazza produces the best mosaic pieces today; hand- or machine-made, they arrive in a palette for easy assembly.

bath

HAPPY LIVING IS LIVING FREE, PERHAPS NOWHERE MORE THAN IN THE BATHROOM – ESPECIALLY IN HOT LANDS, WHERE WE CRAVE TO WASH AWAY SWEAT AND TROUBLE, EMERGING COOL AND COMFORTABLE.

This custom-design is a first for my eyes: a double-length bath for two to sit opposite each other. A lovely idea, but large baths use masses of water, unlike showers; think of the environment and ensure there are two of you in a bath this big.

A bathroom mirror provides time for reflection, both visually and contemplatively, pure white surroundings emptying the mind as the shower cleanses the body. This circular mirror has its fellow by shape in the circular shower rail.

"**G**ood God! To have a room of one's own with a real fire and books and tea and company, and no dinner bells and distractions, and a little time for doing something! It is a wonderful vision, and surely worth some risks."

At first glance you may think this manifesto, which became emblematic of the loose circle of friends known as the Bloomsbury Group in early-20th-century London, is an extract from Virginia Woolf's now famous feminist tract of 1926, *A Room of One's Own*, in which she describes women's oppression in terms of denied space. It is, in fact, the words of Lytton Strachey in a 1909 missive to Duncan Grant, which expresses the longing of the two homosexual men to escape the conventions of bourgeois domesticity they found just as stifling as did their female counterparts. *A Room of One's Own* eventually became a symbol for the struggle to create a more enabling form of domesticity associated with modern life. It was unpredictably the shared emphasis on domesticity that bound the women and men of Bloomsbury into a community more cohesive than more avant-garde groupings of the time.

To feel stifled in any sense is abhorrent, and in the modern world there should be no need for isolation, unless chosen, nor pressure, which is rarely chosen, and I suppose if there is a room that has